毎日
Continue Studying English Every Day!
続ける!
英語リーディング2

・速読編・

木村達哉 著

三省堂

はじめに

　皆さん、こんにちは。木村達哉です。この本を手に取ってくださってありがとうございます。この本は速読ができなくて悩んでいる人のために書きました。

　どうして速く読めないのでしょうか。まずは、語彙力が低く、前後から推測しながらでないと読めないというのが第1の理由です。そしてもう1つは、構造を意識しながらでないと、場合によっては行間にSやVなどの記号を書いたりスラッシュを引いたりしながらでないと、文章が読めないということが挙げられます。この2点を克服すると、あなたは文章を速く読めるようになります。

　この本では、制限時間内で問題を解いていただきます。行間に構造を表す記号などを書きこまず、スマホで日本語を読むように「筆者の言いたいこと」のみに意識を集中させて読んでください。普段から書きこむ習慣ができている人は、その習慣を排除しようとがんばってください。また、復習があなたの語彙力を高めますので、音読を重ねて日本語を英語に直すバックトランスレーションまで行ってください。語彙力が、そして英語力が、驚くほど高くなります。

　トレーニングを続けられるよう、QRコードからアクセスできる動画の中で、継続するためのメッセージを発信しています。必ずチェックし、勉強方法を知るだけでなく、挫折しないようにしてくださいね。

　続ければ必ず点数が伸びます。最後までこの本の指示にしたがって、トレーニングを続けていってください。応援しています。　　　　　木村達哉

目次

専用アプリで音声無料ダウンロード

書名を選んでクラウドマークをタップ！

Webでも音声を無料で提供しています。
https://tb.sanseido-publ.co.jp/gakusan/mainichi-r/ ▶

本書の構成

本書は、DAY1〜14までの全14レッスンから成り、2週間であなたのリーディング力を飛躍的にアップさせる教材です。まずは、各レッスンの学習予定日を書き入れ、その計画通りに学習を進めましょう。また、各レッスンの終わりには著者のワンポイントアドバイス動画もついていますので、毎日の学習の締めくくりに見てみよう。

Question

英文を読み、きちんと内容を把握できたか確認しよう。また、目標時間を目安にとりくもう。

学習予定日 ／ 学習日 ／

まずは全レッスンの学習予定日を書き入れ、その通りに学習を進めよう。

DAY 1

学習予定日 ／ 学習日 ／

Question

▶次の英文を読んで、問いに答えなさい。

目標時間一覧
読む時間 3分
解く時間 1分

Let's say you're talking to someone. Do you know that there is a big difference between the attitude you take when the other person is your close friend and the attitude you take when the other person is someone you don't like? You might be surprised to learn that you are subconsciously changing your posture.

When two friends meet and talk about an open-ended topic, they often have similar attitudes. When those two people are particularly close and feel the same way about the topic they are talking about, their attitudes are often quite similar. They become so similar that they could almost be said to be copies of each other. When one crosses his legs, the other crosses his legs. When one of them starts touching his hair, the other one puts his hands on his head. They are not deliberately imitating each other. They are doing it subconsciously as an expression of natural companionship through gestures.

Why do two people adopt a similar posture? Because the relationship between them is strengthened by the body's silent message, "See, I'm just like you, right?" Strangely enough, even though the message is sent unconsciously, the other person subconsciously understands it fully. It is fair to say that when two people meet face to face, the equality between them is strengthened by the similarity of their attitudes.

On the other hand, when the two people are not so close, they will often adopt completely different postures. If you are especially wary of the other person, you will fold your arms or keep your head down as if you had to defend yourself. And that silent message is also conveyed to the other person, so he becomes increasingly wary of you as well. So, when you don't know a person well and you want to get close to him or her, it's a good idea to observe the person closely and try to adopt a similar attitude.

(注) attitude (体の) 姿勢　　posture 姿勢　　wary 用心深い

① 次の①〜⑤の英文が本文の内容に一致している場合はT、一致していない場合はFを（ ）内に書き入れなさい。

① Discussing a common topic is a way to get to know each other.
（　　　）

② You should notice that you consciously change your posture when talking with your friends.
（　　　）

③ When we are wary of the person we are talking to, we adopt a defensive posture.
（　　　）

④ If the two people talking are close friends, their postures tend to be similar.
（　　　）

⑤ If you don't like the person you are talking to, you tend to end the conversation quickly.
（　　　）

スラッシュを引きながら読むと、スピードが落ちるぞ！

6　　　7

【解答・解説】
前ページの Question の答え合わせをしよう。間違えた問題は、英文の内容について、きちんと把握できていなかった箇所なので、解説を読んでしっかり理解しよう。

【英文訳】
英文の和訳を見て、筆者の言いたいことをきちんと読み取れていたか確認しよう。

Mission 1
英文をしっかりと理解した後で、Question にある英文を見ながら音読トレーニングを行おう。

Mission 2
英文を脳にしっかりと刷り込んだら、最後の仕上げに、前のページにある日本語を見ながら英語にできるか確認しよう。

ワンポイントアドバイス
著者からのワンポイントアドバイス動画が見られるよ。毎日の学習の締めくくりに見てみよう。

DAY 1

Question

▶次の英文を読んで、問いに答えなさい。

目標時間
読む時間：3分
解く時間：1分

Let's say you're talking to someone. Do you know that there is a big difference between the attitude you take when the other person is your close friend and the attitude you take when the other person is someone you don't like? You might be surprised to learn that you are subconsciously changing your posture.

When two friends meet and talk about an open-ended topic, they often have similar attitudes. When those two people are particularly close and feel the same way about the topic they are talking about, their attitudes are often quite similar. They become so similar that they could almost be said to be copies of each other. When one crosses his legs, the other crosses his legs. When one of them starts touching his hair, the other one puts his hands on his head. They are not deliberately imitating each other. They are doing it subconsciously as an expression of natural companionship through gestures.

Why do two people adopt a similar posture? Because the relationship between them is strengthened by the body's silent message, "See, I'm just like you, right?" Strangely enough, even though the message is sent unconsciously, the other person subconsciously understands it fully. It is fair to say that when two people meet face to face, the equality between them is strengthened by the similarity of their attitudes.

On the other hand, when the two people are not so close, they will often adopt completely different postures. If you are especially wary of the other person, you will fold your arms or keep your head down as if you had to defend yourself. And that silent message is also conveyed to the other person, so he becomes increasingly wary of you as well. So, when you don't know a person well and you want to get close to him or her, it's a good idea to observe the person closely and try to adopt a similar attitude.

（注）attitude（体の）姿勢　　posture 姿勢　　wary 用心深い

Q 次の①～⑤の英文が本文の内容に一致している場合は T、一致していない場合は F を（　　）内に書き入れなさい。

① Discussing a common topic is a way to get to know each other.

（　　　　）

② You should notice that you consciously change your posture when talking with your friends.

（　　　　）

③ When we are wary of the person we are talking to, we adopt a defensive posture.

（　　　　）

④ If the two people talking are close friends, their postures tend to be similar.

（　　　　）

⑤ If you don't like the person you are talking to, you tend to end the conversation quickly.

（　　　　）

> スラッシュを
> 引きながら読むと、
> スピードが落ちるぞ！

解答・解説

Q 解答 ① F ② F ③ T ④ T ⑤ F

....

Q 解説

① 「共通の話題を議論することは、お互いを知るための方法である」という意味。本文中に「お互いを知るための方法」についての記述はないので不適当。

② 「友人と話しているときに姿勢を意識して変えていることに気づくべきである」という意味。第 1 段落に You might be surprised to learn that you are subconsciously changing your posture. とあるので、「意識して変えている」という部分が不適当。また「気づくべき」という記述はない。

③ 「話し相手を警戒しているとき、身を守る姿勢をとる」という意味。最終段落に If you are especially wary of the other person, you will fold your arms or keep your head down as if you had to defend yourself. とあり、この部分に一致する。

④ 「話している二人が親しい友人である場合、彼らの姿勢は似る傾向にある」という意味。第 2 段落に When two friends meet and talk about an open-ended topic, they often have similar attitudes. とあり、この部分に一致する。

⑤ 「話している相手が好きでない場合、すぐに会話を終わらせようとしがちである」という意味。好きでない相手についての記述は最終段落に書かれているが、「すぐに会話を終わらせようとしがち」という記述は見られない。

英文訳

　あなたが誰かと話をしているとしよう。相手が親しい友人である場合にとる姿勢と、相手が好きではない人である場合にとる姿勢とでは、大きい違いがあることを知っているだろうか。無意識のうちに自分の姿勢を変えていることを知って、驚くかもしれない。

　二人の友達が会って打ち解けた話をするとき、似たような姿勢をとることが多い。その二人が特に親しく、話している話題に対して同じ気持ちでいるときには、両者の姿勢はかなり似ていることが多い。彼らはほとんどお互いをコピーで写したと言ってもよいほど似てくるのである。片方が足を組むと、もう片方も足を組む。片方が髪を触り始めると、もう片方も手を頭にやる。彼らは故意にお互いを真似ているわけではない。身ぶりによる自然な親交の表現として、無意識に行っているのである。

　なぜ二人は似たような姿勢をとるのであろうか。体が「ほら、僕は君とそっくりだろう？」という無言のメッセージを発することで、二人の関係性が強化されるからである。無意識にメッセージを送っているにもかかわらず、不思議なことに相手はそれを無意識のうちに十分理解しているのである。二人が直接会っているときに、それぞれの姿勢を似せることで、お互いの対等性が強化されると言ってもよいだろう。

　一方、二人がそれほど親しくないときには、両者は全く違う姿勢をとることが多い。特に相手を警戒しているときには、腕を組んだり頭を低くしたりして、自分を守らなければならないかのような姿勢をとる。そして、その無言のメッセージもまた相手に伝わるので、相手もますますあなたを警戒するようになるのである。したがって、相手のことをよく知らず、親しくなりたいと思ったときには、相手をよく観察して、同じような姿勢をとるようにしてみるとよいだろう。

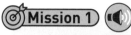

Mission 1 🔊

▶ **Question の英文を見ながら、音読トレーニングをしよう。**

音読トレーニング ▶ □ □ □ □ □ □ □ □ □ □

Mission 2

▶ **前ページの英文訳を見ながら、バックトランスレーションをして、内容を しっかりマスターできたか確認しよう。**

Let's _____ you're talking to _____. Do you _____ that there is a _____ _____ between the _____ you _____ when the other_____ is your close _____ and the _____ you take when the other _____ is _____ you _____ like? You might be _____ to learn that you are subconsciously _____ your _____.

When two _____ meet and _____ _____ an open-ended _____, they often _____ _____ attitudes. When _____ two people are particularly _____ and _____ the same way about the _____ they are _____ about, their _____ are often quite _____. They _____ so similar that they could _____ be said to be _____ of _____ other. When one _____ his legs, the other _____ his legs. When one of them _____ _____ his hair, the other one _____ his _____ on his _____. They _____ _____ deliberately imitating _____ _____. They are _____ it subconsciously as an _____ of natural companionship

10

_____ gestures.

Why do _____ _____ adopt a _____ posture? Because the _____ between _____ is strengthened _____ the body's _____ _____, "See, I'm just _____ you, right?" Strangely _____, even though the _____ is _____ unconsciously, the other person subconsciously _____ it fully. It is _____ to say that _____ two people _____ _____ to _____, the equality _____ them is strengthened by the _____ of their attitudes.

_____ the _____ hand, when the _____ people are _____ so _____, they will often _____ completely _____ postures. _____ _____ are especially wary of the _____ person, you will _____ your arms or _____ your head down _____ _____ you had to _____ yourself. And that _____ message is also _____ to the _____ person, so he _____ increasingly wary _____ _____ as well. So, when you don't know a person _____ and you want to _____ _____ to him or her, it's a good _____ to _____ the person closely and _____ to _____ a similar _____.

リーディングの勉強法や
モチベーションの上げ方を
知りたい人はこちら▶▶▶
https://tb.sanseido-publ.co.jp/gakusan/mainichi-r/

Question

▶次の英文を読んで、問いに答えなさい。

目標時間
読む時間：3分
解く時間：1分

In the Stone Age, our ancestors hunted to survive. They hunted huge mammoths by working with other humans to survive. Today, the need to hunt to survive has disappeared, but our natural animal instincts have not disappeared, and we have an alternative to hunting. Any alternative satisfies our animal instincts as long as it includes the element of defeating a difficult enemy.

For those of us who are fortunate, our daily work is very similar to primitive hunting in that it gives us a sense of fulfillment. Immediate and long-term goals are set, brainstorming is done, and the entire staff works together to catch the "prey." Leaders inspire their staff and when they succeed, they take home a "prey" that is perfect in quantity and quality. They are modern-day hunters, leaving their homes in the morning to go to work, as if saying to their families, "Wait for a while, and I'll bring home a prize in the evening."

For many people, however, work is too hard, boring and repetitive to be an alternative to hunting. Many jobs do not provide the rewarding experience of catching prey, and therefore do not give us an experience that satisfies our instincts. Many people who find work boring and would prefer not to do it become frustrated and stressed out, and some become physically and mentally ill.

Such people have to find "prey" to satisfy their instincts. For many people, if there is a lack of job fulfillment, such a lack can only be made up for by developing a hobby or some other kind of personal passion. Some people regard playing a musical instrument well as "prey," some consider improving their golfing skills as "prey," and others think of defeating a powerful enemy in a computer game as "prey." In short, many people who engage in hobbies are still trying to satisfy their remaining animal instincts.

（注）instinct 本能　　alternative 代用物　　prey 獲物

Ⓠ 次の①～⑤の英文が本文の内容に一致している場合は T、一致していない場合は F を（　）内に書き入れなさい。

① We have lost the instinct to hunt animals, but some people see their work as prey.

（　　　）

② Any alternative can satisfy our instincts but only if it includes the factor of defeating enemies.

（　　　）

③ Work is fulfilling for almost all of us, so it is similar to primitive hunting.

（　　　）

④ For many people, work is not an alternative to hunting.

（　　　）

⑤ For many people, developing a hobby allows them to satisfy their animal instincts.

（　　　）

Q 解答 ①F ②T ③F ④F ⑤T

....

Q 解説

① 「私たちは動物を狩ろうとする本能を失ったが、仕事を獲物だとみなしている人もいる」という意味。第1段落に the need to hunt to survive has disappeared, but our natural animal instincts have not disappeared とあるので不適当。

② 「敵を倒すという要素が含まれていさえすれば、どんな代替物も本能を満たすことができる」という意味。第1段落最終文に Any alternative satisfies our animal instincts as long as it includes the element of defeating a difficult enemy. とあるので、この部分に一致している。

③ 「われわれはほとんどみんな仕事から充足感を得るので、仕事は原始的な狩りに似ている」という意味。第3段落に For many people, however, work is too hard, boring and repetitive to be an alternative to hunting. とあるので、一致しない。

④ 「多くの人にとって、仕事は狩りの代わりにはならない」という意味。第3段落に work is too hard, boring and repetitive to be an alternative to hunting とはあるので、一致している。

⑤ 「多くの人にとって、趣味を深めることで動物的本能を満たすことができる」という意味。本文の最終段落の内容に一致する。

英文訳

　石器時代、われわれの祖先は生き残るために狩りをしていた。巨大なマンモスを、他の人間と協力しながら狩り、そして生き延びていたのである。現代では生き延びるために狩猟をする必要性は消滅したが、生来の動物的な本能は消えておらず、狩猟の代わりとなるものを手に入れているのである。難敵を倒すという要素を含んでいる限り、どのような代用物であっても動物的本能を満たしてくれる。

　恵まれた人々にとっては、毎日の仕事は充実感を与えてくれるという点で、原始的な狩猟に非常に近いものである。目先の目標と長期的目標を設定し、ブレーンストーミングがなされ、スタッフ全員が協力して「獲物」を捕らえる。リーダーたちはスタッフを鼓舞し、成功した暁には量的にも質的にも申し分のない「獲物」を家に持ち帰ることになる。彼らは現代の狩人であり、家族に「夕方にはほうびを持って帰るから待っていなさい」と言うがごとく、朝自宅を出て仕事場に向かうのである。

　しかし、多くの人々にとっては、仕事はあまりにもきつくて退屈で反復的なものであり、狩猟の代用物にはなり得ない。多くの仕事は獲物を捕らえたときのやりがいを与えてはくれず、したがって本能が満たされる経験をすることはない。仕事が退屈で、できることならやりたくないと考える多くの人々は、いらいらしたりストレスが溜まったりして、なかには肉体的にも精神的にも病気になってしまう人もいる。

　そういう人たちは本能を満たす「獲物」を見つけなければならない。多くの人々にとって、仕事の充実感が欠如しているのであれば、そうした欠如は趣味または何らかの個人的に熱中できるものを深めることによってのみ、埋め合わせることができる。楽器をうまく演奏することを「獲物」とする人もいれば、ゴルフが上達することを「獲物」とする人もいれば、コンピューターゲームの中で強敵を倒すことを「獲物」とする人もいる。手短に言えば、趣味に打ち込む多くの人は、依然として残っている自身の動物的本能を満たそうとしているのである。

Mission 1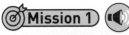

▶ Question の英文を見ながら、音読トレーニングをしよう。

音読トレーニング ▶ □ □ □ □ □ □ □ □ □ □

Mission 2

▶前ページの英文訳を見ながら、バックトランスレーションをして、内容を
しっかりマスターできたか確認しよう。

In the _____ _____, our _____ hunted to _____. They hunted huge mammoths by _____ with _____ humans to _____. Today, the _____ _____ hunt to survive has disappeared, but our _____ animal instincts _____ not disappeared, and _____ have an alternative to _____. Any alternative _____ our _____ instincts as _____ as it includes the _____ of defeating a difficult _____.

For those of _____ who are _____, our _____ work is very _____ to primitive hunting in that it _____ us a _____ of fulfillment. Immediate and long-term _____ are _____, brainstorming is _____, and the _____ staff _____ together to catch the "prey." Leaders _____ their staff and when they _____, they take _____ a "prey" that is perfect in _____ and _____. They are modern-day _____, leaving their _____ in the morning to go to _____, as if saying to their _____, "Wait for a _____, and I'll _____ home a _____ in the _____."

For many people, _____, work is _____ hard, _____ and repetitive to _____ an alternative to _____. Many _____ do not _____ the rewarding experience of _____ prey, and therefore do not _____ us an experience that _____ our _____. Many people who _____ work _____ and would _____ not to do _____ become _____ and _____ out, and some become physically and mentally _____.

Such people have to _____ "prey" to satisfy their _____. For many people, if there is a _____ of _____ fulfillment, such a _____ can only be _____ up for by _____ a hobby or some other kind of personal _____. Some people _____ _____ a musical instrument well _____ "prey," _____ _____ improving their golfing skills as "prey," and _____ think of defeating a _____ enemy in a computer game as "prey." In _____, many people who _____ _____ hobbies are still _____ to _____ their remaining animal _____.

学習予定日　／　　学習日　／

Question

▶次の英文を読んで、問いに答えなさい。

目標時間
読む時間：3分
解く時間：1分

Do you know the law of inertia in physics? When no force is added to an object, or even if it is, when the combined force is zero, an object in motion will continue to move while an object that has stopped will continue to stop. For example, if a train starts suddenly, the passengers are likely to fall backward. In contrast, when a train comes to a sudden stop, the passengers are likely to fall forward. These reactions are both due to the law of inertia.

This law seems to apply to human behaviors as well. That is, people who do something habitually usually try to keep doing it, while people who spend their time doing nothing try to maintain that state. For example, those who jog every day may have started doing so as a way to lose weight or stay fit, but as they are running habitually after a while, they will run for the sake of running itself without realizing it. If you play computer games every day, you'll find out how difficult it is to stop the habit. On the other hand, if you don't work to improve your listening skills every day, it will be difficult to make it a habit. The reason is that you will try to continue to stop according to the law of inertia.

It's great when students who haven't studied hard change their mind one day and start studying. However, it is extremely difficult to keep it up. The only way to stay motivated is to make an effort every day, even if it's just for a short time daily. If you have even one blank day, there's a good chance you'll go back to your original state. Continue to make 20 or 30 minutes of effort every day, and it will become harder and harder to stop, and you will not feel that you are trying so hard, even though people around you might regard you as a hard worker.

（注）the law of inertia 慣性の法則

Q 次の①～⑤の英文が本文の内容に一致している場合は T、一致していない場合は F を（　）内に書き入れなさい。

① The law of inertia is the basis of physics and must be learned well.

（　　　）

② Stopping what you keep doing every day is difficult.

（　　　）

③ There is much evidence that the law of inertia applies to human behaviors.

（　　　）

④ Those who have not been working to improve their listening skills in English find it difficult to start that work.

（　　　）

⑤ By continuing a certain behavior every day, it becomes natural for you to do it.

（　　　）

音読回数が少ないと、
英語力は伸びないぞ！

Q 解答　①F　②T　③F　④F　⑤T

⋯⋯

Q 解説

① 「慣性の法則は物理学の基礎であり、しっかり学ばねばならない」という意味。本文中に、慣性の法則を学ぶべきという記述は見られないので不適当である。

② 「日々続けていることを止めることは難しい」という意味。第2段落に people who do something habitually usually try to keep doing it とあり、その後でゲームを毎日続けている人が止めるのは難しいという例が挙げられているので、この部分に一致する。

③ 「慣性の法則が人間の行動にも当てはまるという証拠が多く存在する」という意味。第2段落に「あてはまるように思われる」と書かれているが、推測の域を出ておらず、「証拠が存在する」という記述は見られない。

④ 「英語のリスニング力向上にとりくんでこなかった人が、そのとりくみを始めるのは難しい」という意味。第2段落にリスニングに関する記述はあるが、it will be difficult to make it a habit（それを習慣にすることは難しい）と言っているのであって、「始める」ことについては書かれていない。

⑤ 「ある行為を日々続けることで、それをすることが自然になる」という意味。第2段落のジョギングの例や最終段落の最終文から判断すると、本文の内容として適当だとわかる。

あなたは物理学における慣性の法則を知っているだろうか。物体に力が加わらないとき、あるいは加わっていてもその合力が0であるとき、動いている物体は動き続けようとし、止まっている物体は止まり続けようとする。たとえば、列車が急発進すると乗客は後方に倒れそうになる。逆に列車が急停止すると、乗客は前方に倒れそうになる。これらの反応はどちらも慣性の法則によるものである。

人間の行動にもこの法則があてはまるように思われる。つまり、習慣的に何かをしている人はふつうそれを続けようとするし、何もしないで時間を過ごしている人はその状態を維持しようとするものである。たとえば、毎日ジョギングをしている人は、当初はダイエットや健康維持を目的として始めたかもしれないが、しばらく習慣的に走っているうちに、自分でも気づかないうちに走ることそのもののために走るようになる。コンピューターゲームを毎日している人は、その習慣を止めることがいかに難しいかわかるだろう。逆に、あなたがリスニング力を向上させるよう毎日とりくまなければ、それを習慣にすることは難しい。なぜならば、あなたは慣性の法則にしたがって、止まり続けようとするからである。

勉強をあまり熱心にしてこなかった生徒が、ある日に気持ちを切り替えて勉強を始めるのは素晴らしいことである。しかし、それを続けることは極めて難しい。モチベーションを維持するためには、1日あたり短時間でもよいので、毎日努力をするしかない。1日でも空白の日をつくってしまうと、元の状態に戻ってしまう可能性が高いのである。毎日20分でも30分でも努力し続けていれば、今度はそれを止めることがどんどん難しくなってくるし、周囲の人からは努力家だとみなされるかもしれないが、自分はそれほど頑張っているという感覚をもたなくなるだろう。

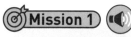
▶ **Question の英文を見ながら、音読トレーニングをしよう。**

音読トレーニング ➤ □ □ □ □ □ □ □ □ □ □

Mission 2

▶ 前ページの英文訳を見ながら、バックトランスレーションをして、内容を
しっかりマスターできたか確認しよう。

　　　Do you ＿＿＿＿＿ the ＿＿＿＿＿ of inertia in physics? When no force is ＿＿＿＿＿ to an ＿＿＿＿＿, or even if it is, when the ＿＿＿＿＿ force is zero, an object ＿＿＿＿＿ ＿＿＿＿＿ will continue to ＿＿＿＿＿ while an object that has ＿＿＿＿＿ will continue to ＿＿＿＿＿. For example, if a ＿＿＿＿＿ ＿＿＿＿＿ suddenly, the ＿＿＿＿＿ are likely to ＿＿＿＿＿ backward. In ＿＿＿＿＿, when a ＿＿＿＿＿ comes to a sudden ＿＿＿＿＿, the passengers are likely to ＿＿＿＿＿ ＿＿＿＿＿. These ＿＿＿＿＿ are both ＿＿＿＿＿ to the law of inertia.

　　　This law ＿＿＿＿＿ to ＿＿＿＿＿ to human behaviors as well. That is, people who do ＿＿＿＿＿ habitually usually try to ＿＿＿＿＿ doing it, while people who ＿＿＿＿＿ their time ＿＿＿＿＿ nothing try to ＿＿＿＿＿ that state. For example, those ＿＿＿＿＿ jog every day may have ＿＿＿＿＿ doing so as a ＿＿＿＿＿ to ＿＿＿＿＿ weight or ＿＿＿＿＿ fit, but as they are running ＿＿＿＿＿ after a ＿＿＿＿＿, they will run for the

_____ of running itself _____ realizing _____. If you _____ computer games every day, you'll _____ _____ how _____ it is to _____ the habit. _____ the _____ hand, if you don't _____ to _____ your listening skills _____ _____, it will be difficult to _____ it a _____. The _____ is that you will _____ to _____ to _____ _____ to the law of inertia.

It's _____ when students who haven't _____ hard _____ their _____ one day and start _____. However, it is extremely _____ to _____ it _____. The _____ way to stay _____ is to make an _____ every day, even if it's _____ for a _____ time _____. If you have even one _____ _____, there's a _____ _____ you'll go back to your original _____. _____ to make 20 or 30 minutes of _____ every day, and it will become _____ and _____ to stop, and you will _____ _____ that you are _____ so hard, even though people _____ you might _____ you as a hard _____.

リーディングの勉強法や
モチベーションの上げ方を
知りたい人はこちら▶▶▶
https://tb.sanseido-publ.co.jp/gakusan/mainichi-r/

学習予定日　/　　学習日　/

Question

▶ 次の英文を読んで、問いに答えなさい。

目標時間
読む時間：3分
解く時間：1分

There is a place called Nago in northern Okinawa. There is a large aquarium nearby, so many people from all over the world visit the city. Nago Bay is extremely beautiful, with views of Iejima and Minnajima, and on a clear day, the sunset will move you. But, in the past, dolphin fishing used to take place in Nago Bay. During the dolphin fishing season, this beautiful bay was red with dolphin blood.

We don't see a lot of dolphins in Nago Bay now, but there used to be quite a few of them swimming around. It was not known why the dolphins came into the bay, but local fishermen say that the dolphins may have mistakenly thought they were in deep water because of the darkened area in Nago Bay, where the mountains are reflected on the surface of the ocean. When the fishermen saw the dolphins swimming in the bay in alarming numbers, they boarded a boat and led the group to the shallow waters. Nago residents with sticks in their hands were waiting for them to beat them to death. In other words, this dolphin fishing was not only carried out by the fishermen, but by all the citizens of Nago. It may seem cruel, but dolphins were a valuable source of protein for them, and dolphin fishing was a part of Nago's culture and tradition.

Currently, we don't see dolphin fishing in Nago. There are a number of companies that offer whale watching for tourists, and they say you don't see many dolphins in the bay now. However, if you walk around

Nago, you will probably see illustrations of dolphins all over the city. You can see cute dolphins with various expressions on the doors of taxis and the walls of restaurants, and dolphin statues have been built in the city. The dolphins are still an important symbol for the people of Nago.

Q 次の①〜⑤の英文が本文の内容に一致している場合はＴ、一致していない場合はＦを（　）内に書き入れなさい。

① Many people visit Nago City because there is an aquarium nearby.

（　　　　）

② There used to be a time when Nago Bay turned red when the dolphin fishing began.

（　　　　）

③ There was and still is very little chance of seeing dolphins in Nago Bay.

（　　　　）

④ Fishermen caught the dolphins from their fishing boats and provided them for the citizens.

（　　　　）

⑤ Although dolphin fishing is no longer practiced, many dolphin symbols can be seen in Nago.

（　　　　）

自分の力は
自分で伸ばすのだ！
挫折するな！

解答・解説

Q 解答 ①T ②T ③F ④F ⑤T

··

Q 解説

① 「近くに水族館があるので、名護市を訪れる人々は多い」という意味。第1段落に There is a large aquarium nearby, so many people from all over the world visit the city. とあるので、一致する。

② 「イルカ漁が始まると名護湾が赤く染まった時期もあった」という意味。第1段落に During the dolphin fishing season, this beautiful bay was red with dolphin blood. とあるので、一致する。

③ 「名護湾でイルカを見る機会は、昔も今もほとんどない」という意味。第2段落に We don't see a lot of dolphins in Nago Bay now, but there used to be quite a few of them swimming around. とあり、以前は極めてたくさんのイルカがいたことがわかる。quite a few は「非常に多くの」という意味。

④ 「漁師が漁船からイルカを釣り上げ、それを市民に提供した」という意味。第2段落にイルカ漁の様子が書かれているが、漁師がイルカを追い込んで市民が棒で殺していたことがわかる。

⑤ 「もうイルカ漁は行われていないが、名護にはイルカのシンボルがたくさんある」という意味。第3段落に if you walk around Nago, you will probably see illustrations of dolphins all over the city とあり、一致する。

英文訳

　沖縄の北部に名護という場所がある。近くに大きい水族館があって、多くの人々が世界中からその街を訪れる。名護湾は極めて美しく、伊江島や水納島などが見えるし、晴れた日には夕陽が人々の心を動かすことだろう。しかしこの名護湾で、以前はイルカ漁が行われていた。イルカ漁が行われる季節には、この美しい湾がイルカの血で真っ赤に染まったのである。

　現在では多くのイルカを名護湾で見かけることはないが、以前はかなりの数のイルカが泳いでいたのである。どうしてイルカがこの湾に入ってきたのかはわからなかった。しかし、地元の漁師たちによれば、名護湾に山影が海面に映って暗くなる部分があるため、その場所をイルカが深い海だと勘違いしたのではないかということである。おびただしい数のイルカが湾内を泳いでいるのを見ると、漁師たちは船に乗って群れを浅瀬へと誘導した。そこで手に棒を持った名護の住民たちが待ち受けていて、イルカたちを殴り殺したのである。つまり、イルカ漁は漁師たちによってだけでなく、名護の住民総出で行われていたのである。残酷に思えるかもしれないが、イルカは彼らにとって貴重なタンパク源であったし、イルカ漁は名護における１つの文化であり、伝統であったのである。

　現在はイルカ漁を名護で見ることはない。観光客にホエールウォッチングを楽しませる会社は数多くあるが、彼らに聞いても、多くのイルカを湾内で見かけることは今はないということである。しかし、名護市内を歩くと、街のいたるところでイルカのイラストを目にすることであろう。タクシーのドアやレストランの壁などに、さまざまな表情をした可愛いイルカを見ることができるし、イルカの像が街中に建てられている。名護の人々にとっては今もなおイルカが大切なシンボルなのである。

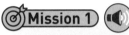

Mission 1 🔊

▶ Question の英文を見ながら、音読トレーニングをしよう。

音読トレーニング ▶ ☐ ☐ ☐ ☐ ☐ ☐ ☐ ☐ ☐ ☐

Mission 2

▶ 前ページの英文訳を見ながら、バックトランスレーションをして、内容を
しっかりマスターできたか確認しよう。

There is a _____ called Nago in _____ Okinawa. There is a large _____ nearby, so many people from _____ _____ the _____ visit the city. Nago Bay is extremely _____, with _____ of Iejima and Minnajima, and on a _____ day, the _____ will _____ you. But, in the _____, dolphin fishing _____ _____ take place in Nago Bay. During the dolphin fishing season, this beautiful bay was _____ with dolphin _____.

We _____ _____ a lot of dolphins in Nago Bay _____, but there used to _____ quite _____ _____ of them swimming _____. It was not _____ _____ the dolphins _____ _____ the bay, but _____ fishermen say that the dolphins may have mistakenly _____ they were in _____ _____ because _____ the darkened area in Nago Bay, where the mountains are _____ on the _____ of the ocean. When the fishermen _____ the dolphins

28

_____ in the bay in alarming _____, they _____ a boat and _____ the group to the _____ waters. Nago residents with _____ in their _____ were _____ for them to _____ them to _____. In _____ _____, this dolphin fishing was not only _____ _____ by the fishermen, but by all the _____ of Nago. It may seem _____, but dolphins were a _____ _____ of protein for _____, and dolphin fishing was a _____ of Nago's _____ and _____.

_____, we _____ _____ dolphin fishing in Nago. There are a number of _____ that _____ whale watching _____ tourists, and they say you _____ _____ _____ dolphins in the bay _____. However, if you _____ _____ Nago, you will probably see illustrations of _____ all _____ the city. You can see cute dolphins _____ _____ expressions on the _____ of taxis and the _____ of restaurants, and dolphin _____ have been _____ in the city. The dolphins are _____ an _____ _____ for the people of Nago.

リーディングの勉強法や
モチベーションの上げ方を
知りたい人はこちら▶▶▶
https://tb.sanseido-publ.co.jp/gakusan/mainichi-r/

DAY 5

Question

▶次の英文を読んで、問いに答えなさい。

目標時間
読む時間：3分
解く時間：1分

　Thanks to the development of the Internet as well as newspapers and books, there is a lot of information around us and we can have easy access to it. At first glance, this seems very convenient. However, some of the information we pick up from all around us can be dangerous, and we can often find ourselves at an extreme disadvantage if we speak or act on such information. It must also be noted that there are not a few people who try to use some of this type of information to their advantage.

　Napoleon is said to have slept only about three hours a day, and it seems that this anecdote is often used by people today in a very educational way. When parents talk to their children about Napoleon, they may tell them that he only slept for a short time in order to achieve great things, and that they should make an effort even if they sleep less in order to realize their dreams. But this message is clearly wrong.

　We can't be certain whether Napoleon slept for only three hours a day, but he certainly seems to have had a small amount of sleep. But we may not say that he made any effort to accomplish anything grand in his waking hours. There are some references which say he took a bath for about six hours a day (a quarter of the day) and rubbed his whole body with a dry cloth after his bath. Considering that he would be in his bathroom while we were sleeping in our beds, and that he would be in bed for about three hours while we were working, we may even say that we are making a much greater effort than Napoleon.

To be sure, even if most of us had lived in Napoleon's time, we probably would not have been able to clean up the mess that followed the French Revolution, nor would we have been able to put under control most of the European nations other than Britain, Russia and the Ottoman Empire. But to believe the anecdote that Napoleon slept for only a short time and worked hard, and to tell our children to be like a person who established a military dictatorship is a foolish educational approach that is based only on biased information.

（注）anecdote 逸話、エピソード　　mess 混乱

　　　a military dictatorship 軍事独裁政権

Q **次の①～⑤の英文が本文の内容に一致している場合は T、一致していない場合は F を（　）内に書き入れなさい。**

① A lot of people attempt to use incorrect information to their advantage.

（　　　）

② It is factually incorrect that Napoleon slept only about three hours a day.

（　　　）

③ Having too much knowledge is dangerous for education.

（　　　）

④ Napoleon bathed six hours a day, so it is not quite true that he worked harder than we do.

（　　　）

⑤ It is educationally wrong to use the anecdote about Napoleon to make children work harder.

（　　　）

Q 解答　①F　②F　③T　④T　⑤T

....

Q 解説

① 「誤った情報を自分の有利になるように使おうとする人が多い」という意味。第1段落の最終文に there are not a few people who try to use some of this type of information to their advantage とあるので、内容に一致する。

② 「ナポレオンが日に約3時間しか寝ていなかったというのは事実に反している」という意味。第3段落に We can't be certain whether Napoleon slept for only three hours a day, but he certainly seems to have had a small amount of sleep. とあるので、日に約3時間しか睡眠時間がなかったというのが完全に間違った情報とは言えない。したがって不適当。

③ 「あまりにも知識があり過ぎるのは教育にとって危険である」という意味であるが、本文中にそういった記述は見られない。

④ 「ナポレオンは日に6時間風呂に入っていたので、彼が我々より努力していたとはあながち言えない」という意味。第3段落の最終文に we may even say that we are making a much greater effort than Napoleon とあるので、内容に一致する。not quite は部分否定を表し「完全に～というわけではない」という意味。

⑤ 「子どもにもっと努力させるためにナポレオンの逸話を用いるのは教育的に間違っている」という意味。本文の最終文に、ナポレオンの逸話を使うことを a foolish educational approach that is based only on biased information だと述べているので、内容に一致する。

英文訳

　新聞や書物だけでなく、インターネットが発達したおかげで、われわれの周囲にはたくさんの情報があり、われわれは気軽にそれを利用することができる。一見すると非常に便利である。しかし、あちこちで拾った情報の中には危険なものもあり得るため、それに基づいて発言したり行動したりすると、極めて不利な立場に追い込まれかねないことはよくある。また、この種の情報の一部を自分に有利になるように利用しようとする人々がかなり多いことにも注意しておかねばならない。

　ナポレオンは1日に約3時間しか寝なかったと言われていて、このエピソードは現代人によって非常に教育的な意味でよく使われているように思われる。親が子どもにナポレオンについて語るとき、ナポレオンは大きいことを成し遂げるために、ほんの短時間しか眠らなかったのであり、夢をかなえるためには睡眠時間を削ってでも努力すべきであると言うことがあるかもしれない。しかし、このメッセージは明らかに間違っている。

　ナポレオンが1日に3時間しか寝なかったかどうかは確かではないが、確かに睡眠時間は短かったようである。しかし、彼は起きている時間に壮大なことを成し遂げるための努力をしていたとは言えないのではないだろうか。彼は1日に約6時間（1日の4分の1）もの間風呂に入り、風呂上がりには全身を乾布摩擦していたという文献がいくつか残っている。われわれが寝ている間、彼は風呂に入り、われわれが働いている間に彼は3時間ほど寝ていたと考えれば、ナポレオンよりもわれわれのほうがかなり頑張っていると言うことさえできるのではないだろうか。

　確かに、われわれの多くがナポレオンの時代に生きていたとしても、おそらくフランス革命後の混乱を収拾することなどできなかったし、イギリス・ロシア・オスマン帝国以外のヨーロッパのほとんどの国を勢力下に置くこともできなかったであろう。しかし、ナポレオンは短時間しか寝ずに熱心に働いたというエピソードを信じて、軍事独裁政権を築き上げた彼のようになるように子どもたちに言うことは、偏った情報のみに基づいた愚かな教育法である。

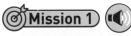

Mission 1 🔊

▶ **Question の英文を見ながら、音読トレーニングをしよう。**

音読トレーニング ▶ ☐ ☐ ☐ ☐ ☐ ☐ ☐ ☐ ☐ ☐

Mission 2

▶ **前ページの英文訳を見ながら、バックトランスレーションをして、内容を しっかりマスターできたか確認しよう。**

_____ to the _____ of the Internet as _____ as newspapers and books, there is _____ _____ _____ information _____ us and we _____ _____ easy _____ to it. At _____ _____, this seems very _____. However, some of the information we _____ _____ from all around us _____ _____ dangerous, and we can often _____ _____ at an extreme disadvantage if _____ _____ or _____ on _____ information. It _____ also be _____ that there are not _____ _____ people who _____ to _____ some of this type of information to their _____.

Napoleon is _____ to have _____ only about three hours a _____, and it _____ that this anecdote is often used by people today in a very _____ _____. When parents _____ _____ their children about Napoleon, they may _____ them that he _____ slept _____ a _____ time in order to _____ great _____, and that they _____ _____ an _____ even if they _____ less in order to _____ their dreams. But this _____ is clearly _____.

We can't be _____ whether Napoleon _____ for _____ three hours a day, but he _____ seems to have had a small _____ of sleep. But _____ _____ not say that he _____ any _____ to accomplish anything grand in his _____ _____. There are some _____ which say he _____ a _____ for about six hours a _____ (a _____ of the day) and _____ his whole body with a dry cloth _____ _____ _____. Considering that he _____ _____ in his bathroom while we _____ _____ in our beds, and that he would _____ _____ _____ for about three hours while we were _____, we _____ _____ _____ that we are making a _____ _____ effort _____ Napoleon.

To _____ _____, even if most of us had _____ in Napoleon's _____, we probably would not have been _____ to _____ up the mess that _____ the French Revolution, _____ would we have been able to _____ under _____ _____ of the European _____ _____ _____ Britain, Russia and the Ottoman Empire. But to _____ the anecdote that Napoleon _____ for only a short time and _____ hard, and to tell our children _____ _____ _____ a person who _____ a military dictatorship is a _____ educational _____ that is _____ only on _____ information.

リーディングの勉強法や
モチベーションの上げ方を
知りたい人はこちら▶▶▶
https://tb.sanseido-publ.co.jp/gakusan/mainichi-r/

Question

▶次の英文を読んで、問いに答えなさい。

目標時間
読む時間：3分
解く時間：1分

A famous Japanese playwright has stated that the decline in Japan's birth rate has a lot to do with the fact that the number of skiers is decreasing. At first glance, the birth rate and the number of skiers seem to have nothing to do with each other. But if you think carefully about what he is saying, there may be more than a few people who think that he is not necessarily wrong. If you've ever been to a ski resort, you may know what he means. There are so many couples who fall in love at ski resorts. There are a lot of couples who fall in love on the ski slopes, and there are also quite a few couples who keep in touch with each other after returning to their hometowns from the resorts. Ski resorts are a place for men and women to meet.

In order to ski, you need to have time and money to spare. For modern people, who are running out of both of these things, going skiing on their days off is a bit of a luxury. So, it's no surprise that the number of skiers is decreasing. In addition, the number of ski resorts is decreasing because of the lack of snow due to global warming. The playwright says that these are reasons that have caused young people to have fewer opportunities to meet each other (and, of course, fall in love), with the result that the birth rate in Japan has fallen.

There is no knowing if he's right or not, but as the saying goes, "It's an ill wind that blows nobody any good," some factors that seem completely unrelated are often closely related. For example, the downturn in the world's economy and historical incidents are often linked to unexpected causes, which surprises historians. What matters is, when a serious problem arises, you should not try to find only one cause or reason. If you look for causes from all perspectives, you can find some unexpected causes as well as surprising solutions to problems.

（注）playwright 劇作家

Q 次の①～⑤の英文が本文の内容に一致している場合は T、一致していない場合は F を（　）内に書き入れなさい。

① Without doubt, the decline in Japan's birth rate is linked with the decrease in skiers.

（　　　）

② Those who have skied might understand the playwright's point of view.

（　　　）

③ People without time or money to spare are unable to have children.

（　　　）

④ It is just because there are fewer skiers that the number of ski resorts has decreased.

（　　　）

⑤ Often there are interrelationships between seemingly unrelated factors.

（　　　）

解答・解説

Q 解答　①F　②T　③F　④F　⑤T

．．．

Q 解説

① 「間違いなく、日本の出生率の低下はスキーをする人が減っていることに関係がある」という意味。第1段落において、ある劇作家の意見として、出生率の低下とスキーをする人が減っていることに関係があると述べているが、最終段落の最初に There is no knowing if he's right or not とあるので、「間違いなく」という部分が一致しない。

② 「スキーをしたことがある人は劇作家の言い分を理解するかもしれない」という意味。第1段落に If you've ever been to a ski resort, you may know what he means. とあるので一致する。

③ 「時間もお金も余裕がない人は子どもをつくることができない」という意味。第2段落に For modern people, who are running out of both of these things, going skiing on their days off is a bit of a luxury. とはあるが、子どもをつくることができないという記述はない。

④ 「スキー場の数が減ったのは、単にスキーをする人が少なくなったからである」という意味。第2段落に the number of ski resorts is decreasing because of the lack of snow due to global warming とあるので一致しない。

⑤ 「関係がないと思われる要素間に相互関係があることが多い」という意味。最終段落に some factors that seem completely unrelated are often closely related とあるので、この部分に一致する。

英文訳

　日本のある有名な劇作家が「日本の出生率が落ちているのは、スキーをする人が減っていることと大いに関係がある」と述べている。一見すると出生率とスキーをする人の数は、互いにまったく関係がないように思える。しかし、彼の言っていることをよく考えてみると、必ずしも間違いとは言えないと思う人も少なからずいるのではないだろうか。スキー場に行ったことのある人なら、彼の言わんとしていることがわかるかもしれない。スキー場で恋に落ちるカップルは非常に多い。ゲレンデで恋に落ちて、スキー場からそれぞれの故郷に戻ったあとに連絡をお互いに取り続けるというカップルも非常に多い。スキー場というのは男女の出会いの場なのである。

　スキーをするためには、時間的余裕と経済的余裕が必要である。その両方がなくなりつつある現代人にとって、休みの日にスキーに行くというのは、ちょっとした贅沢なのである。だからスキーをする人が減っているのも当然で、それに加えて地球温暖化による雪不足のために、スキー場の数が減少しつつある。当の劇作家が言うには、これらの理由で若者がお互いに出会う（そしてもちろん、恋に落ちる）機会が減ることになり、結果として日本の出生率が落ちてしまったのである。

　彼が正しいかどうかはわからない。しかし、「誰の得にもならない風は吹かない（風が吹けば桶屋が儲かる）」という言葉があるように、まったく関係のないように見える要素が実は密接に関係しあっていることが多い。たとえば、世界の経済状況の悪化にしても、歴史的な事件にしても、思いもよらない原因と結びついていることが多く、歴史家を驚かせる。大切なのは、重大な問題が生じたとき、ひとつの原因や理由だけを追究しようとしてはいけないということである。ありとあらゆる視点から原因を探してみると、問題の驚くべき解決法だけでなく、予想もしないような原因も見えてくるのである。

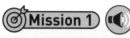

Mission 1 🔊

▶ **Question の英文を見ながら、音読トレーニングをしよう。**

音読トレーニング ▶ ☐ ☐ ☐ ☐ ☐ ☐ ☐ ☐ ☐ ☐

Mission 2

▶ **前ページの英文訳を見ながら、バックトランスレーションをして、内容を しっかりマスターできたか確認しよう。**

A _____ Japanese playwright has _____ that the _____ in Japan's _____ _____ has a lot to _____ _____ the fact that the number of _____ is decreasing. At first _____, the birth rate and the _____ of skiers _____ _____ have _____ to do with _____ _____. But if you _____ _____ about what he _____ _____, there _____ _____ more than _____ _____ people who _____ that he is not necessarily _____. If you've _____ been to a ski _____, you may _____ what he _____. There are _____ _____ couples who _____ _____ love at ski resorts. There are a lot of _____ who fall in _____ on the ski slopes, and there are _____ _____ a few couples who _____ in _____ with each other _____ returning to their _____ from the _____. Ski resorts are _____ _____ for men and women to _____.

_____ _____ _____ ski, you _____ to have _____ and _____ to spare. For _____ people, who are _____ out of both of these things, going _____ on their _____ off is a _____ of a luxury. So, _____ _____ _____ that the number of skiers is _____. _____ _____, the number of ski resorts is decreasing _____ _____ the lack of snow _____ _____ global _____. The playwright _____ that these are _____ that have _____ young people to have _____ opportunities to _____ each other (and, of course, fall in love), with the _____ that the _____ rate in Japan has _____.

There is _____ _____ if he's right or not, but as the saying _____, "It's an _____ _____ that blows _____ any good," some _____ that seem completely _____ are often _____ related. _____ _____, the downturn in the world's _____ and historical _____ are often _____ _____ unexpected _____, which surprises historians. _____ _____ is, when a _____ problem arises, you _____ _____ try to _____ only one _____ or reason. If you _____ _____ causes from _____ perspectives, you can find some _____ _____ as well as surprising _____ to problems.

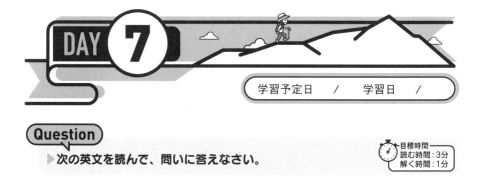

学習予定日　　/　　学習日　　/

Question
▶次の英文を読んで、問いに答えなさい。

目標時間
読む時間：3分
解く時間：1分

Over the years, writing an autobiography has become popular. Not only famous people but even ordinary citizens write about what has happened to them from their birth to the present day on SNS or weblogs. Needless to say, ordinary people cannot get a publisher to publish what they have written, but they write long autobiographies on Facebook or other SNS, which many people don't even read.

However, it seems that most people have a very hard time writing their autobiographies. Why is it so difficult for people to write their own history? The most likely reason is that they want to write about something but do not know what to write about, so they write about themselves. Based on the premise that what you know best is what you can write about best, it would not be surprising to think that you would be able to write best about yourself because you think you know yourself best. But unfortunately, the premise of this syllogism is doubtful. Can you really write well about what you know best? Try reading a book on English written by a university professor who specializes in English, and you will find that there is so much information in it that even the simplest things are difficult to understand. It's not that what you know best can be written best. A little knowledge is certainly dangerous, but excessive knowledge is also a barrier to clear understanding.

The second reason why you cannot write your autobiography well is that you don't always know yourself well. Why do so many people spend so much time consulting psychiatrists and medical counselors? Why do so many people go on a "journey of self-discovery"? It is very difficult to express your hidden self in writing. In addition, as you are conscious that someone will read your autobiography, you end up trying to make yourself look better, which may result in writing many lies.

（注）autobiography 自伝　premise 前提　syllogism 三段論法
phychiatrist 精神科医

Q 次の①〜⑤の英文が本文の内容に一致している場合は T、一致していない場合は F を（　）内に書き入れなさい。

① While writing autobiographies has become popular, many people cannot write well.

（　　　）

② Even if you write your autobiography on SNS, hardly any people will read it.

（　　　）

③ It's not so difficult to put into writing what you know best.

（　　　）

④ Nothing is more difficult to read than an English book written by an English expert.

（　　　）

⑤ We don't actually know ourselves very well, so it's hard to put ourselves in writing.

（　　　）

Q **解答** ①T ②T ③F ④F ⑤T

....

Q **解説**

① 「自伝を書くことが人気であるが、多くの人がうまく書けないでいる」という意味。第１段落に writing an autobiography has become popular とあり、第２段落に most people have a very hard time writing their autobiographies とあるので、内容に一致する。

② 「自伝を SNS に書いたとしても、ほとんど読まれることはない」という意味。第１段落に they write long autobiographies on Facebook or other SNS, which many people don't even read とあるので、内容に一致する。

③ 「一番よくわかっていることを文章化するのはそれほど難しくない」という意味。第２段落に It's not that what you know best can be written best. とあるので一致しない。

④ 「英語の専門家が書いた英語の本ほど読みにくいものはない」という意味。第２段落に Try reading a book on English written by a university professor who specializes in English, and you will find that there is so much information in it that even the simplest things are difficult to understand. とはあるが、それが最も読みにくいという記述はなく、内容に一致しない。

⑤ 「人は実は自分のことをよくわかっているわけではないので、自分のことを文章化するのは難しい」という意味。第３段落に you don't always know yourself well とあり、また It is very difficult to express your hidden self in writing. とあるので、一致する。

英文訳

　何年も前から自伝を書くことが人気である。有名な人たちのみならず、一般市民でさえも、SNS やブログに自分が生まれてから今日までどんなことがあったのかを書いている。言うまでもなく、ふつうの人々の場合、書いたものを出版社から出版することなどできないが、フェイスブックや他の SNS に長々と、多くの人は読むことさえないのに、自伝を書いているのである。

　しかし、自伝を書くことに非常に苦労している人がほとんどであるように思われる。どうして自分の歴史を書くのがそんなに難しいのであろうか。もっともありそうな理由としては、そもそも文章を書いてみたいが何を書いてよいのかわからないので、自分について書いているということがある。一番よく知っていることが一番うまく書けるという前提に基づけば、自分のことは一番よく知っていると思っているので、自分のことが一番うまく書けるはずだと考えても驚くことではないであろう。ところが残念ながら、この三段論法は、その前提が疑わしい。一番よく知っていることを本当にうまく書けるものなのだろうか。英語を専門としている大学教授が書いた英語の本を読んでみるとよい。そうすれば、あまりにも情報が多過ぎて、どんなに簡単なことであっても理解することは難しいとわかるだろう。一番よく知っていることが一番うまく書けるというわけではないのである。生半可な知識は確かに危険だが、過剰な知識もまた、明確な理解への障壁でもある。

　自伝がうまく書けない2つ目の理由としては、人は自分のことを必ずしもよくわかっているわけではないということである。どうしてそんなにも多くの人々が精神科医や医療カウンセラーに相談するのに長い時間を費やすのであろうか。どうして多くの人々が「自分探しの旅」に出かけるのであろうか。隠された自分を文章で表現するのは非常に難しいのである。また、自伝を誰かに読んでもらうことを意識すると、自分をよりよく見せようとして、結果として多くの嘘を書くことになりかねないのである。

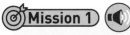

Mission 1 🔊

▶ Question の英文を見ながら、音読トレーニングをしよう。

音読トレーニング ➡ ☐ ☐ ☐ ☐ ☐ ☐ ☐ ☐ ☐ ☐

Mission 2

▶ 前ページの英文訳を見ながら、バックトランスレーションをして、内容を
しっかりマスターできたか確認しよう。

_____ _____ _____, writing an autobiography has become _____. _____ _____ famous people _____ even ordinary citizens write about _____ _____ _____ to them from their _____ to the present _____ on SNS or weblogs. _____ _____ _____, ordinary people cannot get a publisher _____ _____ what they have _____, but they write long autobiographies _____ Facebook or other SNS, which many people don't _____ _____.

However, it seems that _____ _____ have a very _____ _____ writing their autobiographies. Why is it so _____ for people to _____ their own _____? The most _____ _____ is that they _____ _____ write about _____ but do not know _____ _____ write about, so they write about _____. _____ _____ the premise that _____ you know _____ is _____ you can _____ about best, it would not be _____ to _____ that you would be able to write _____

about _____ because you think you know yourself _____.
But unfortunately, the _____ of this syllogism is _____.
Can you really write _____ about _____ you know _____?
_____ reading a book on English _____ by a university
_____ who specializes _____ English, and you will _____
that there is so _____ information in it that even the _____
things are difficult to _____. It's not that _____ you
_____ best can be _____ best. A _____ knowledge is
certainly _____, but excessive knowledge is also a _____ to
_____ understanding.

   The _____ reason why you cannot _____ your autobiography
_____ is that you don't _____ _____ yourself well. Why
do so many people _____ so much _____ consulting
psychiatrists _____ medical counselors? Why do so many
people _____ _____ a "journey of self-discovery"? It is very
difficult to _____ your _____ self in _____. _____
_____, as you are conscious that someone will _____ your
autobiography, you _____ _____ trying to _____ yourself
_____ _____, which may _____ _____ writing many
_____.

リーディングの勉強法や
モチベーションの上げ方を
知りたい人はこちら▶▶▶
https://tb.sanseido-publ.co.jp/gakusan/mainichi-r/

Review 1 DAY 1~7で学習した単語や表現を復習しよう。

☐	development	名 発展、発達	▶DAY 5
☐	needless to say	言うまでもなく	▶DAY 7
☐	stay fit	健康を維持する	▶DAY 3
☐	biased	形 偏見をいだいて	▶DAY 5
☐	relationship	名 関係、仲	▶DAY 1
☐	in contrast	対照的に	▶DAY 3
☐	imitate	動 真似る	▶DAY 1
☐	doubtful	形 疑わしい、はっきりしない	▶DAY 7
☐	resident	名 住民	▶DAY 4
☐	decline	動 減少する、低下する	▶DAY 6
☐	extremely	副 極めて、極端に	▶DAY 3
☐	achieve	動 達成する、やり遂げる	▶DAY 5
☐	alarming	形 驚くべき	▶DAY 4
☐	fulfillment	名 満足（感）	▶DAY 2
☐	subconsciously	副 無意識に	▶DAY 1
☐	accomplish	動 成し遂げる、達成する	▶DAY 5
☐	hidden	形 隠れた、秘められた	▶DAY 7
☐	aquarium	名 水族館	▶DAY 4
☐	unexpected	形 予期しない、思いがけない	▶DAY 6
☐	quite a few	かなり多数の人（物）	▶DAY 4
☐	repetitive	形 繰り返しの	▶DAY 2
☐	at first glance	一見したところでは	▶DAY 6
☐	satisfy	動 満足させる、喜ばせる	▶DAY 2
☐	deliberately	副 故意に、わざと	▶DAY 1
☐	birth rate	出生率	▶DAY 6

コラム 1～興味の幅を広げよう！～

　どうすれば速読できるようになるのですか。僕は2020年の新型コロナウィルス感染症のパンデミックによって全国の学校が休校になった際にYouTube のチャンネル（キムタツチャンネル）を立ち上げました。それ以来、全国の先生方や生徒たち、保護者の皆さんからの質問に答えていますが、高校生から最初に届いた質問が速読の方法を教えてほしいというものでした。皆さんならその質問にどう答えますでしょうか。

　日本語を読む際も同じことが言えるのですが、内容が頭に入ってこないと速く読めないですよね。かといって驚くほどの速度で目を動かしても（そういうトレーニングもないわけではないですが）理解できなければまったく意味がありません。理解するためには、コンテンツに対する興味がないといけません。加えて、文章内で用いられている語彙や表現の知識がないと理解できません。

　以上のことから、大切なことは「コンテンツへの興味＋語彙力」であるとわかるはずです。たとえば、野球が好きな人が野球についてのコラムを読むとします。コンテンツ（野球）に興味があり、使われている語彙の知識もあれば、すらすらと読めますよね。その人が園芸についてのコラムを読むとします。コンテンツ（園芸）に対する興味も、使われている語彙の知識も不足しているという場合、なかなか目が前に進まないはずです。模試などで興味のある内容の文章が出題され、やった！という気持ちになった経験のある人もおられるのではないでしょうか。

　でもなかなか興味のある文章には出会わないですよね。その点で言えば、普段から多くの文章に触れて、興味をもとうとすることは大切です。そして1つでも多くの語彙や表現を覚えようとしてください。それを「毎日続ける！」という姿勢があれば、速読力が驚くほど伸びていきます。挫折しないでください。毎日続けてください。

Question

▶次の英文を読んで、問いに答えなさい。

目標時間
読む時間：3分
解く時間：1分

Many Japanese people think that they are not good at English, but they still believe that they can read English sentences and write about something in English. They believe that they can read and write in English, even though they cannot understand foreigners speaking in English or speak about something in English. This is because in Japan, most of the English classes in schools spend a lot of time and energy on reading and writing. Even if English teachers emphasize English listening and speaking, reading and writing skills are necessary to pass the exams because the majority of university entrance exams are based on reading and writing. Therefore, it is assumed that any Japanese who has graduated from a university can read and write English.

However, this is generally a wrong way of thinking. If you can read in English, you should be able to read English newspapers and magazines at will. However, it seems that few Japanese people can read them without English dictionaries. In addition, research shows that even their ability to read texts written in Japanese is declining. How can they read texts in foreign languages when they cannot even read well in their mother tongue?

Also, if you can write in English, you should also be able to speak it. For example, you should be able to write freely in your native language about your daily life, about the features of your school or workplace, or about the places you have visited. Then try to see if you can speak the same thing in your mother tongue. If you can write about it, then you can speak about it as long as there are no problems with your vocal cords, right? The reason why Japanese people cannot speak English is that they cannot write in English. In other words, most Japanese people are not only unable to listen to or speak English, but they are also not good at reading or writing English sentences.

（注）vocal cords 声帯

🅠 次の①〜⑤の英文が本文の内容に一致している場合は T、一致していない場合は F を（　）内に書き入れなさい。

① Thanks to English education, Japanese people are good at reading and writing English.

（　　　）

② In Japan, more English teachers emphasize English listening and speaking.

（　　　）

③ Most Japanese cannot read English newspapers and magazines, even with a dictionary.

（　　　）

④ Many Japanese cannot speak English because they are not good at writing in English.

（　　　）

⑤ As long as you can write a sentence, it is natural that you can say the same thing.

（　　　）

解答・解説

Q 解答　①F　②F　③F　④T　⑤T

....

Q 解説

① 「英語教育のおかげで、日本人は英語の読み書きが得意である」という意味。第1段落に they still believe that they can read English sentences and write about something in English とはあるが、第2段落と第3段落でそれを否定している。

② 「日本では英語のリスニングとスピーキングに重点を置く英語教員が増えている」という意味。第1段落に Even if English teachers emphasize English listening and speaking とはあるが、このような教員が増えているという記述は見られない。

③ 「ほとんどの日本人は辞書を使っても、英字新聞や雑誌を読むことができない」という意味。第2段落に few Japanese people can read them without English dictionaries とあるので一致しない。

④ 「多くの日本人は、英語で書くのが苦手なので英語を話すことができないのである」という意味。第3段落に The reason why Japanese people cannot speak English is that they cannot write in English. とあるので一致する。

⑤ 「文を書くことができるなら、同じことが話せるのは当然である」という意味。第3段落に If you can write about it, then you can speak about it とあるので一致する。

英文訳

　日本人の多くは英語を苦手だと考えているが、それでも英語の文章を読んだり、英語を使って何かを書いたりすることはできると思っている。外国人が英語で話しているのを理解したり、英語で何かについて話したりすることはできないが、英語で読むことと書くことはできると信じているのである。なぜなら日本において、学校の英語の授業の多くが読むことと書くことに多くの時間とエネルギーを使うからである。英語教員が英語のリスニングとスピーキングを重視したとしても、大学入試問題の大部分が読むことと書くことを基本としているので、試験に合格するためには読み書きの能力が必要になる。したがって、大学を卒業した日本人であれば、英語を読むことと書くことはできると考えているのである。

　しかし、それは概して間違った考え方である。もしも英語で読むことができるのであれば、英字新聞や雑誌を自由に読みこなしているはずである。しかし、それらを英語の辞書なしで読むことができる日本人はほとんどいないだろう。それに加えて、調査によれば、日本語で書かれた文章を読む力さえ低下していることが示されている。母語でさえもうまく読めないのであれば、どうやって外国語の文章を読めるというのだろう。

　また、英語で書くことができるのであれば、話すこともできるはずである。たとえば、母語で自分の日常生活について、自分の学校や職場の特徴について、自分が訪れた場所について、自由に書けるだろう。そして同じ内容を母語で話せるかどうかを試してみればよい。書けるのであれば、声帯に問題がない限り話せるはずではないか。日本人が英語を話せないのは、英語で文章を書くことができないからである。つまり、日本人の多くは英語を聞いたり話したりすることができないだけでなく、英語の文章を読むことも書くことも苦手なのである。

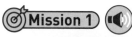

Mission 1 🔊

▶ Question の英文を見ながら、音読トレーニングをしよう。

音読トレーニング ▶ ☐ ☐ ☐ ☐ ☐ ☐ ☐ ☐ ☐ ☐

Mission 2

▶ 前ページの英文訳を見ながら、バックトランスレーションをして、内容を
しっかりマスターできたか確認しよう。

Many Japanese people _____ _____ they are _____

_____ at English, but they _____ _____ that they

_____ _____ English sentences and _____ _____

something _____ English. They _____ that they can

_____ and _____ in English, _____ _____ they cannot

_____ foreigners _____ in English or _____ about

something in English. _____ _____ _____ in Japan, most

of the _____ _____ in schools _____ a lot of _____ and

_____ on _____ and _____. Even if English teachers

_____ English listening and speaking, reading and writing

_____ are _____ to _____ the exams because the _____

of university _____ _____ are _____ _____ reading and

writing. _____, it is assumed that _____ _____ who has

_____ _____ a university can _____ and write English.

However, this is _____ a _____ way of _____. If you

can read in English, you _____ be able to _____ English

newspapers and _____ at _____. However, it seems that _____ Japanese people _____ read them _____ English dictionaries. _____ _____, research _____ _____ even their _____ to read _____ written in Japanese is _____. How can they read texts _____ _____ languages when they cannot _____ _____ well in their mother _____?

Also, if you can _____ in English, you _____ also be _____ to _____ it. For _____, you should be able to write _____ in your _____ language about your _____ _____, about the features of your _____ or _____, or about the places you _____ _____. Then _____ _____ see if you can _____ the same thing in your mother _____. If you can _____ about it, then you can _____ about it _____ _____ _____ there are _____ _____ with your vocal cords, _____? _____ _____ why Japanese people cannot _____ English is that they cannot _____ in English. _____ _____ _____, most Japanese people are _____ only _____ to listen to _____ speak English, _____ they are also _____ _____ at reading _____ writing English sentences.

学習予定日　／　学習日　／

Question

▶次の英文を読んで、問いに答えなさい。

目標時間
読む時間：3分
解く時間：1分

There are a lot of schools in Japan that have a rule that students are not allowed to bring their smartphones into school. Even in those schools that allow it, teachers often instruct students to turn them off in school and not to turn them on until they get out of the school gate. Smartphones, needless to say, are extremely useful tools, not only for searching for information, but also for helping students study English and math. Since teachers want their students to study hard, you would think that they would encourage the use of smartphones more. In reality, a lot of schools still prohibit their use. What is the reason for this?

The first reason is gaming. In May 2019, the World Health Organization officially recognized "gaming disorder," a condition in which excessive gaming makes daily life difficult, as an international disease. With the spread of smartphones, the problem of gaming addiction has become more serious, and there is growing concern that it could be harmful to health. It is believed that schools, as places of learning, should not allow students to bring the source of this problem into the classroom. If smartphones are allowed to be brought to school, the number of students playing games during class or breaks will surely increase, no matter how strict the teachers' instructions may be.

Another reason lies in the problem of cyberbullying. Quite a few students are unable to come to school due to cyberbullying through

SNS. This type of bullying is now considered one of the most serious problems in Japanese schools. It seems that, in the past, most bullying was done through physically harming weaker students, but today, most bullying is Internet-related. It would therefore not be wrong to instruct students not to bring smartphones, which could cause such a serious problem, into school. Smartphones are convenient, but if users misunderstand their purpose, it is only natural that their use should be limited.

（注）disorder 異常、病気

Q 次の①～⑤の英文が本文の内容に一致している場合は T、一致していない場合は F を（　）内に書き入れなさい。

① It is not good that many schools in Japan do not let students bring their smartphones to school.

（　　　）

② Some schools in Japan let you bring your smartphone to school if you switch it off until you leave school.

（　　　）

③ Teachers want students to study, so they should allow them to bring their smartphones to school.

（　　　）

④ Some students will play games even during class if they bring their smartphones to school.

（　　　）

⑤ The number of students who can't come to school because of cyberbullying is decreasing.

（　　　）

解答・解説

解答　①F　②T　③F　④T　⑤F

....

解説

① 「日本の多くの学校が生徒たちにスマートフォンの学校への持ち込みを許していないのはよくない」という意味。第1段落で There are a lot of schools in Japan that have a rule that students are not allowed to bring their smartphones into school. とあるが、これに対して筆者がよくないと思っている記述は見られない。

② 「学校を出るまで電源を切るなら、スマートフォンを学校に持ってきてもかまわないという学校も日本にある」という意味。第1段落で Even in those schools that allow it, teachers often instruct students to turn them off in school and not to turn them on until they get out of the school gate. とあるので、この部分に一致する。

③ 「教員は生徒たちに勉強してほしいのだから、スマートフォンの学校への持ち込みを許すべきである」という意味。第1段落に Since teachers want their students to study hard, you would think that they would encourage the use of smartphones more. とはあるが、持ち込みを許すべきだと筆者が述べているわけではない。

④ 「学校にスマートフォンを持ち込むと、授業中でもゲームをする生徒がいるだろう」という意味。第2段落に If smartphones are allowed to be brought to school, the number of students playing games during class or breaks will surely increase とあり、一致している。

⑤ 「ネットいじめのために学校に来られない生徒の数は減少傾向にある」という意味。第3段落に Quite a few students are unable to come to school due to cyberbullying through SNS. とあるので一致しない。

英文訳

校則で生徒がスマートフォンを学校に持参することを禁じている学校が日本には多い。それを許している学校であっても、学校の中では電源を切って、校門を出るまでは電源を入れないように教員が指導しているところが多い。スマートフォンは言うまでもなく、極めて便利なツールであり、情報を検索するだけでなく、生徒が英語や数学の勉強をする助けとなる。教員は生徒に熱心に勉強してほしいと願っているのだから、スマートフォンの使用をもっと促してもよいのではないかと思われるが、実際には使用を禁止している学校が依然として多いのである。その理由は何なのだろうか。

1つ目の理由はゲームである。2019年5月、世界保健機関は、ゲームのやり過ぎで日常生活が困難になる「ゲーム障害」を国際疾病として正式に認定した。スマートフォンの普及でゲーム依存の問題が深刻化し、健康を害する懸念は強まっているのである。その元凶を生徒が教室に持ち込むことを、学びの場である学校が認めるべきではないと考えられている。もし、スマートフォンを学校に持ってくることを許可すれば、いくら教員が厳しく指導したとしても、授業中や休み時間にゲームをする生徒が必ず増えるだろう。

もう1つの理由は、インターネットを通じたいじめ問題にある。SNSを使ったいじめにより、学校に来ることができない生徒がかなりいる。この種類のいじめは今、日本の学校においてはもっとも重大な問題のひとつとみなされているのである。過去においては弱い生徒に身体的ダメージを負わせるいじめが多かったようだが、現代ではほとんどのいじめがインターネット関連なのである。それゆえ、そのような深刻な問題を引き起こしかねないスマートフォンを学校に持ってこないように生徒を指導するのは、間違いではないだろう。スマートフォンは便利ではあるが、使い手がその目的を間違えてしまうと、使用を制限されるべきなのは極めて当然である。

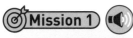

Mission 1 🔊

▶ Question の英文を見ながら、音読トレーニングをしよう。

音読トレーニング ➡ ☐ ☐ ☐ ☐ ☐ ☐ ☐ ☐ ☐ ☐ ☐

Mission 2

▶ 前ページの英文訳を見ながら、バックトランスレーションをして、内容を
しっかりマスターできたか確認しよう。

_____ _____ a lot of schools in Japan that _____ a
_____ that students are _____ _____ to _____ their
smartphones into _____. Even in those schools that _____
_____, teachers _____ instruct students to _____ them
_____ in school and _____ to _____ them _____ until
they _____ _____ of the school _____. Smartphones,
_____ _____ _____, are extremely _____ tools, not only
for _____ for information, but also for _____ students
_____ English and math. Since teachers _____ their
students to study _____, you would _____ that they would
_____ the use of smartphones _____. In _____, a lot of
schools still _____ their use. _____ is the _____ for this?

The _____ _____ is gaming. In May 2019, the World
Health Organization officially recognized "gaming disorder," a
_____ in which excessive _____ makes _____ life _____,
as an international _____. _____ the _____ of

smartphones, the _____ of gaming addiction _____ _____ more _____, and there is _____ concern that it could be _____ to _____. It is believed that schools, as _____ of _____, should not _____ students to _____ the source of this _____ into the classroom. _____ smartphones are _____ to be _____ to school, the number of students playing games during _____ or _____ will surely _____, _____ _____ _____ strict the teachers' _____ may be.

_____ reason _____ in the problem of cyberbullying. _____ a few students are _____ to come to school _____ _____ cyberbullying _____ SNS. This type of _____ is now _____ one of the most _____ problems in Japanese _____. It seems that, in the past, most bullying _____ _____ through physically _____ weaker students, but today, _____ bullying is Internet-related. It would therefore not be _____ to instruct students _____ to _____ smartphones, which could _____ _____ a serious problem, into school. Smartphones are _____, _____ if users misunderstand their _____, it is only _____ that their _____ should be _____.

リーディングの勉強法や
モチベーションの上げ方を
知りたい人はこちら▶▶▶
https://tb.sanseido-publ.co.jp/gakusan/mainichi-r/

Question

▶次の英文を読んで、問いに答えなさい。

There are many different creatures on earth, but only humans laugh. Some zoologists claim that there are animals that laugh, but there are no creatures that laugh like humans do. Laughter is a kind of language. No matter where you are in the world, people laugh in almost the same way, so even if you don't speak the same language or think differently, you can strengthen the bonds of your hearts by smiling at each other. It has also been scientifically proven that laughter plays a role as a kind of medicine. Laughter improves blood circulation and lowers blood pressure and heart rate. Laughter seems to be one of the most powerful weapons we have, but why do we laugh?

Some people might say that we laugh because something is funny. That's not wrong, but we must remember we laugh when we are surprised, when we are happy, and sometimes while we are crying. Imagine a birthday party, for example. You are in your own home, surrounded by your family. All of you are smiling and having a good time. Just then, you hear a loud noise like a pistol outside your house! Startled, you open the curtains and look out into the yard to see your friend there, setting off a firecracker. You are relieved and will begin to laugh as the tension of surprise disappears. Sometimes when we see an amazing object or action, we can't help but smile the moment we realize it is not dangerous.

Evolutionary theory suggests that laughter is a response to the absence of danger or to the passing of danger. Perhaps primitive people laughed at each other to confirm that the danger had passed. You smile because you know there is no danger at a birthday party, and you smile because you know that loud noises do not necessarily mean danger. It is reasonable to think that laughter in the middle of crying is an effort to get out of a difficult situation somehow. If you were to watch TV dramas and movies from this perspective, it would be very interesting to observe why actors laugh in connection with danger.

（注）blood circulation 血行　　blood pressure 血圧　　heart rate 心拍数

Q 次の①～⑤の英文が本文の内容に一致している場合は T、一致していない場合は F を（　）内に書き入れなさい。

① Some animals laugh like humans do, but no animals laugh when they are funny.

（　　　　）

② Even in areas with different languages and cultures, people laugh in almost the same way.

（　　　　）

③ If you're surprised at something, you start laughing when you realize there's no danger.

（　　　　）

④ The reason you laugh when you are sad is that you are trying to get out of that situation.

（　　　　）

⑤ Producers of dramas and movies seem to know the relation between laughter and danger.

（　　　　）

解答・解説

Q 解答 ①F ②T ③T ④T ⑤F

··

Q 解説

① 「人間のように笑う動物もいるが、おもしろいときに笑う動物はいない」という意味。第1段落に there are no creatures that laugh like humans do とあるので一致しない。

② 「言葉と文化が違う地域であっても、人間はほとんど同じように笑う」という意味。第1段落に No matter where you are in the world, people laugh in almost the same way とあるので一致している。

③ 「何かに驚いても、危険がないとわかると笑い始める」という意味。第2段落に will begin to laugh as the tension of surprise disappears とあり、この部分に一致している。

④ 「悲しいときに笑う理由は、その状況を脱しようとしているのである」という意味。第3段落に It is reasonable to think that laughter in the middle of crying is an effort to get out of a difficult situation somehow. とあるので一致している。

⑤ 「ドラマや映画のプロデューサーは笑いと危険の関係を知っているように思われる」という意味だが、このような記述は本文中にはない。

英文訳

　地球上にはさまざまな生き物がいるが、笑うのは人間だけである。笑う動物もいると主張する動物学者もいるが、人間のように笑う生き物は存在しない。笑いは一種の言語である。世界のどの地域であっても、人間はほとんど同じように笑うので、言葉が通じなくても、あるいは考え方が違っても、笑顔を交わすことで心のきずなを強めることができるのである。また、笑いは一種の薬の役割を果たしていることが科学的に証明されている。笑うことで血行がよくなったり血圧や心拍数が下がったりするのである。笑いは人間のもつ最強の武器のひとつであるように思われるが、なぜわれわれは笑うのであろうか。

　何かがおもしろいから笑うのだという人もいるかもしれない。それは間違いではないが、しかしわれわれは驚いたときにも楽しいときにも、時には泣いているときにも笑うことを忘れてはならない。たとえば誕生日パーティーを想像してほしい。あなたは自分の家にいて、家族に囲まれている。家族はみな笑顔で楽しいひと時を過ごしている。そのときに家の外でピストルのような大きい音がする！　驚いたあなたがカーテンを開けて庭を見ると、あなたの友達がそこにいて、クラッカーを鳴らしたのである。あなたはホッとすると同時に、驚きの緊張が解けて笑い始めるだろう。われわれは驚くべき物や行為を目の当たりにすると、それが危険でないとわかった瞬間に思わず笑顔になってしまうことがある。

　進化論が示唆するのは、笑いは危険がないこと、あるいは危険が過ぎ去ったことに対する反応だということだ。おそらく原始人は危険が過ぎ去ったのを確認するために互いに笑い合ったのだろう。誕生日パーティーでは危険などないことがわかっているから笑顔になるし、大きい音が必ずしも危険を意味しないことがわかったから笑顔になるのである。泣いている最中に笑う場合も、なんとかしてその困難な状況を脱しようとする努力だと考えれば合理的である。その観点でテレビドラマや映画を見れば、俳優がどうして笑顔になるのかを危険との関連において観察すると、非常に興味深いことだろう。

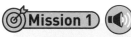

Mission 1 🔊

▶ Question の英文を見ながら、音読トレーニングをしよう。

音読トレーニング ▶ ☐ ☐ ☐ ☐ ☐ ☐ ☐ ☐ ☐ ☐

Mission 2

▶ 前ページの英文訳を見ながら、バックトランスレーションをして、内容を
しっかりマスターできたか確認しよう。

There are many different _____ on _____, but _____
humans _____. Some zoologists _____ that there are _____
that _____, but there are _____ _____ that laugh _____
humans _____. Laughter is a _____ _____ language. _____
_____ _____ you are in the _____, people laugh _____
_____ the same _____, so even if you _____ _____ the
_____ language or _____ differently, you can strengthen the
_____ of your _____ by _____ at each _____. It has _____
_____ scientifically _____ that laughter _____ a _____ as a
kind of _____. Laughter _____ blood circulation and _____
blood _____ and heart _____. _____ seems to be one of the
most _____ weapons we _____, but _____ do we _____?

　Some people _____ _____ that we _____ because
something is _____. That's _____ _____, but we must
_____ we laugh when we are _____, when we are _____,
and sometimes _____ we are _____. _____ a birthday

party, _____ _____. You are _____ your own _____, surrounded by your _____. All of you are _____ and having a _____ time. _____ _____, you hear a _____ noise _____ a pistol _____ your house! Startled, you _____ the curtains and _____ out _____ the yard to _____ your friend there, setting off a firecracker. You _____ _____ and will begin to _____ as the tension of _____ _____. Sometimes when we see an _____ _____ or action, we _____ _____ but smile the _____ we realize it is _____ dangerous.

Evolutionary _____ suggests that _____ is a _____ to the _____ of danger or to the _____ of _____. _____ primitive people _____ _____ each other to _____ that the danger had _____. You _____ because you know there is _____ _____ at a birthday party, and you _____ because you know that _____ _____ do not necessarily mean _____. It is _____ to think that laughter in the _____ of _____ is an _____ to get out of a _____ situation _____. If you _____ _____ _____ TV dramas and movies from this _____, it would be very interesting to _____ why actors _____ in connection with _____.

リーディングの勉強法や
モチベーションの上げ方を
知りたい人はこちら▶▶▶
https://tb.sanseido-publ.co.jp/gakusan/mainichi-r/

DAY 11

Question

▶次の英文を読んで、問いに答えなさい。

目標時間
読む時間：3分
解く時間：1分

　How would you respond if someone said to you, "I saw a man-eating tiger in that forest."? Some people might start running away to get away from that forest, while others might curiously run to that forest. Needless to say, the person would have to run away because he or she saw a tiger that has a habit of eating people. However, if you read aloud "I saw a man-eating tiger in that forest," it could also be heard as "I saw a man eating tiger in that forest." So, some people might think the person saw a man who was eating tiger in that forest. However, if you misunderstand the person's remark, your knowledge of English grammar is a little inadequate, which is because the correct English is "I saw a man eating a tiger in that forest."

　There are those who believe that knowledge of English grammar is not so important when learning English. Some even deny the importance of learning by heart as many words and phrases as possible, which is surprising. If you don't know the rules and vocabulary of a language, how will you ever be able to use it? A Japanese person trying to communicate in incorrect English may be treated kindly if the person is just a tourist, but it is extremely annoying to native speakers if the person works or does research in English. You can't do business involving hundreds of millions of dollars with someone who can't speak well, and you can't communicate well with someone who can't communicate properly in research where correct language is important.

If your goal in learning English is to enjoy traveling abroad, you don't need to learn much grammar and vocabulary. You can use gestures and enjoy talking to the local people. However, if your goal in learning English is to work or do research with people from all over the world, you will need to know basic English rules. When reading, writing, and listening to English texts, you have to study them carefully and learn the vocabulary and expressions so that you can use the correct English. Although it is not possible to reach a high level of English immediately, it is important to set a high goal and learn the correct English.

Q 次の①〜⑤の英文が本文の内容に一致している場合は T、一致していない場合は F を（　）内に書き入れなさい。

① If you don't know the rules of English well, you might be in danger when traveling.

（　　　）

② Even if you heard someone say they saw a man eating a tiger, you should not believe it.

（　　　）

③ You must not believe that it's unnecessary to learn English grammar to master English.

（　　　）

④ It is impossible to do business or research with someone who cannot speak well or communicate properly.

（　　　）

⑤ You can't master English instantly, but you should aim high and learn the correct English.

（　　　）

解答・解説

Q 解答　①F　②F　③T　④T　⑤T

⋯⋯⋯⋯⋯⋯⋯⋯⋯⋯⋯⋯⋯⋯⋯⋯⋯⋯⋯⋯⋯⋯⋯⋯⋯⋯⋯⋯⋯⋯⋯⋯⋯

Q 解説

① 「英語のルールをよく知らなければ、旅行中に危険な目に遭うかもしれない」という意味。第3段落に If your goal in learning English is to enjoy traveling abroad, you don't need to learn much grammar and vocabulary. とあり、「危険な目に遭う」という記述は見られない。

② 「人がトラを食べているのを見たと誰かが言うのを聞いたとしても、信じるべきではない」という意味。本文中にはこのような記述がない。

③ 「英語を習得するのに英文法学習は不必要であるということを信じてはいけない」という意味。第2段落に If you don't know the rules and vocabulary of a language, how will you ever be able to use it? とあるので、この部分に一致する。

④ 「しっかりと話したりきちんと意思疎通したりできない人とビジネスや研究をするのは不可能である」という意味。第2段落に You can't do business involving hundreds of millions of dollars with someone who can't speak well, and you can't communicate well with someone who can't communicate properly in research where correct language is important. とあり、一致している。

⑤ 「英語を即座に習得することはできないが、目標を高く掲げて、正しい英語を学ぶべきである」という意味。第3段落最終文に Although it is not possible to reach a high level of English immediately, it is important to set a high goal and learn the correct English. とあるので、一致している。

英文訳

　もしあなたが "I saw a man-eating tiger in that forest." と誰かに言われたら、どのように答えるだろうか。その森から離れるために逃げ始める人がいるかもしれないし、興味をもってその森へと走り出す人がいるかもしれない。言うまでもなく、その人は「人を食べる習性をもつトラを見た」のであるから、逃げ出さねばならないのである。しかし、声に出して "I saw a man-eating tiger in that forest." を読んでみると、"I saw a man eating tiger in that forest." とも聞こえる。だから、その人は森の中でトラを食べている人を見たのだなと思う人がいるかもしれない。ただ、もしその人の発言を誤解するとしたら、英文法の知識が少し不十分である。なぜなら正しい英語は "I saw a man eating a tiger in that forest." だからである。

　英語を学ぶ際に、英文法の知識はそれほど大切ではないと考える人がいる。中には語句をできるだけたくさん覚えることの重要性を否定する人もいることには驚かされる。ある言語のルールも語彙も知らずに、どうやってそれを使いこなすというのだろう。日本人が間違った英語を使ってコミュニケーションをとろうとすると、単なる観光客であれば優しく接してもらえるであろうが、英語を使って仕事をしたり研究をしたりするのであれば、ネイティブスピーカーにとっては極めて迷惑である。しっかりと話せない相手と何億ドルものお金が動くようなビジネスはできないし、正確な言葉が大切な研究においてきちんと意思疎通ができない相手としっかり気持ちを通わせられるはずがないのである。

　英語を学ぶ目的が海外旅行を楽しむことであれば、それほど文法や語彙を学ぶ必要はない。身振り手振りを使いながら、現地の人々と楽しんで話をすることはできるだろう。しかし、もしも英語を学ぶ目的が、世界中の人々と仕事をしたり研究をしたりすることなのであれば、基本的な英語のルールを知っておくことは必要である。英語の文章を読んだり書いたり聞いたりしながら、入念に勉強し、語彙や表現を覚えることで、正しい英語を使えるようになってくる。即座に高いレベルの英語に到達することはできないが、目標を高く掲げて、正しい英語を身につけることが大切なのである。

Mission 1 🔊

▶ Question の英文を見ながら、音読トレーニングをしよう。

音読トレーニング ▶ ☐ ☐ ☐ ☐ ☐ ☐ ☐ ☐ ☐ ☐

Mission 2

▶ 前ページの英文訳を見ながら、バックトランスレーションをして、内容を
しっかりマスターできたか確認しよう。

How _____ you _____ if someone _____ _____ you, "I _____ a _____ tiger in that _____."? Some people _____ start _____ _____ to get away from that _____, while _____ might _____ run to that _____. _____ to say, the person would have to _____ _____ because he or she _____ a _____ that has a _____ of _____ people. However, if you read _____ "I saw a man-eating tiger in that forest," it _____ also be _____ as "I saw a _____ _____ tiger in that _____." So, _____ people _____ think the _____ saw a _____ who was _____ tiger in that forest. However, _____ you misunderstand the person's _____, your _____ of English grammar is _____ _____ inadequate, which is _____ the _____ English is "I saw _____ _____ eating a _____ in that forest."

There are _____ who _____ that knowledge of English grammar _____ _____ so _____ when _____ English. Some even _____ the importance of _____ by _____ as many words and phrases as _____, which is _____. If you _____ _____ the _____ and vocabulary of a language, _____ will _____ ever be able to _____ it? A Japanese person _____ _____ communicate in _____ English may be _____ kindly _____ the person is _____ a _____, but it is extremely _____ to _____ speakers if the person _____ or _____ _____ in English. You can't _____ _____ involving hundreds of _____ of dollars with someone who _____ speak _____, and you _____ communicate _____ with someone who _____ communicate _____ in _____ where correct language is _____.

_____ your _____ in learning English is _____ _____ traveling _____, you don't _____ _____ learn much _____ and vocabulary. You can _____ _____ and _____ _____ to the _____ people. However, if _____ _____ in learning English is _____ _____ or do _____ with people from _____ _____ the _____, you will _____ to _____ basic English _____. When _____, writing, and listening to English _____, you have to _____ them _____ and _____ the vocabulary and _____ so that you _____ use the _____ English. Although it is not _____ to _____ a high level of English _____, it is _____ to _____ a high _____ and learn the _____ English.

リーディングの勉強法や
モチベーションの上げ方を
知りたい人はこちら▶▶▶
https://tb.sanseido-publ.co.jp/gakusan/mainichi-r/

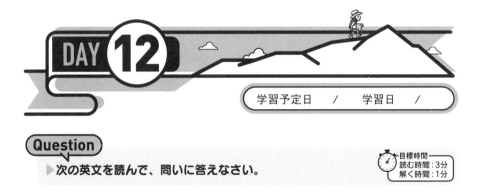

Question

▶次の英文を読んで、問いに答えなさい。

目標時間
読む時間：3分
解く時間：1分

　A lot of parents and teachers in Japan have been telling children for quite some time to read a lot of books to improve their Japanese grades. It goes without saying that books are not meant to be read in order to raise test scores, so authors must feel sad to have their works read for this purpose alone, and it is unlikely that children who are told to read for this reason by adults will read books willingly. I wonder if reading a lot of books will improve their Japanese test scores.

　We should keep in mind that there are three main types of reading. The first type of reading is for pleasure. It is a lot of fun to read mystery novels and try to guess who the criminal is. It is exciting to read *Robinson Crusoe* or *The Adventures of Tom Sawyer* and feel as if you were a character in the novels as you turn the pages. It is also a pleasure to read inspirational essays. Especially, essays written by writers who know a lot about foreign countries can make you feel as if you were living in those places.

　The second type is reading for information. Reading newspapers and magazines is probably the most typical way to get information. Reading a lot of books about the Japanese economy, the American presidential system, or the history of infectious diseases is a way to gain knowledge and information. This type of reading may not be enjoyable, but it is essential for writing reports and giving a presentation at a conference. Besides, it is a vital type of reading for getting highly educated.

Therefore, educated people go to libraries and bookstores to get books filled with various information and knowledge, and try to learn a lot by reading them.

Finally, the third type is reading to improve your ability to express yourself and expand the size of your vocabulary. Whenever you come across an expression you've never read before, you can make a note of it, memorize it, and use it to improve your writing skills the next time you write something. This type of reading helps you follow what the author means in a logical way and gives you the ability to summarize your own opinion on it. This type of reading is what leads to higher scores in Japanese tests. So, if you only focus on the first and second types of reading, your test scores will not be as high as you expect them to be.

Q 次の①〜⑤の英文が本文の内容に一致している場合はT、一致していない場合はFを（　）内に書き入れなさい。

① It is no fun for children to read in order to improve their Japanese scores.

（　　　）

② Reading books for fun leads to reading many books, which improves your test scores.

（　　　）

③ Adventure novels are exciting because they make you feel as if you were a character in the story.

（　　　）

④ Reading to get information may be boring, but it is necessary to become educated.

（　　　）

⑤ Reading to improve expressive powers improves your Japanese scores.

（　　　）

解答・解説

解答　①T　②F　③T　④T　⑤T

∴∴∴

解説

① 「国語の点数を上げるために本を読むのは子どもにとってはおもしろくない」という意味。第 1 段落に it is unlikely that children who are told to read for this reason by adults will read books willingly. とあり、一致する。

② 「楽しみのために本を読むことが多読につながり、テストの点数が上がる」という意味。第 2 段落に楽しみのための読書について書いてあるが、多読につながるという記述はないし、最終段落に if you only focus on the first and second types of reading, your test scores will not be as high as you expect them to be とあるので、テストの点数も上がらないことがわかる。

③ 「冒険小説は登場人物になったかのように感じられてわくわくする」という意味。第 2 段落に feel as if you were a character in the novels とあり、一致する。

④ 「情報を得るための読書はつまらないかもしれないが、教養を身につけるには必要である」という意味。第 3 段落に This type of reading may not be enjoyable とあり、さらに it is a vital type of reading for getting highly educated とあるので、一致する。

⑤ 「表現能力を高める読書が国語の点数を上げる」という意味。このようなタイプの読書についての説明が最終段落にあるが、This type of reading is what leads to higher scores in Japanese tests. とあるので、一致している。

日本にはかなり前から、国語の成績を上げるために本をたくさん読むようにと子どもたちに伝えてきた親や教員が多い。本はテストの成績を上げるために読むものではないことは言うまでもないので、こういったねらいだけのために自分の著作を読まれる作家は悲しく思うだろうし、大人にこういった理由から読書をするように言われた子どもたちが喜んで本を読むとは思えない。本をたくさん読めば国語のテストの成績は上がるのであろうか。

　読書には主に3つの種類があることを覚えておくとよい。1つ目の読書は読んで楽しむ読書である。推理小説を読んで、誰が犯人なのかを推理するのは非常に楽しい。『ロビンソン・クルーソー』や『トム・ソーヤーの冒険』を読んで、自分がまるで小説の登場人物であるかのように感じながらページをめくるとわくわくする。また、心に染み入るエッセイを読むのも楽しい。特に海外事情について詳しい作家が書いたエッセイは、まるで自分がその場所に住んでいるように感じることができる。

　2つ目の読書は情報を得るための読書である。新聞や雑誌の読書は情報を得るためのおそらくもっとも典型的なものであろう。日本経済について、アメリカの大統領制度について、感染症の歴史について、本をたくさん読むのは、知識や情報を得るための1つの方法である。この種類の読書は、楽しめないかもしれないが、論文を書いたり会議でプレゼンをしたりするためには必須である。加えて、高い教養を身につけるためには必要不可欠な読書なのである。したがって、教養のある人たちは図書館や書店でさまざまな情報や知識のつまった本を手にし、それを読むことによってたくさんのことを身につけようとするのである。

　最後に、第3の読書は自己表現力を高めたり、語彙力を拡充するための読書である。それまで読んだことのない表現に出会ったら、その表現をノートに書いたり、記憶したり、文章力を高めるために次に何かを書くときに使用したりすることができる。このような読み方は筆者の言っていることを論理的に追う助けとなり、それに対する自分の意見をまとめる力を与えてくれる。この種類の読書こそが、国語のテストの点数を上げることにつながるのだ。だから、第1と第2の読書だけに集中すると、テストの点数は期待しているほど上がらないのである。

Mission 1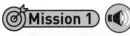

▶ **Question の英文を見ながら、音読トレーニングをしよう。**

音読トレーニング ➡ ☐ ☐ ☐ ☐ ☐ ☐ ☐ ☐ ☐ ☐

Mission 2

▶ **前ページの英文訳を見ながら、バックトランスレーションをして、内容を
しっかりマスターできたか確認しよう。**

A lot of _____ and _____ in Japan have been _____ children _____ quite some time to _____ a lot of books to _____ their Japanese _____. It _____ _____ saying that books are not _____ to be _____ in order to _____ test _____, so _____ must feel _____ to have their _____ read for this _____ _____, and it is _____ that children who are _____ _____ read for this _____ by adults will read books _____. I _____ _____ reading a lot of books will _____ their Japanese test _____.

We should _____ in _____ that there are _____ main _____ of _____. The _____ type of reading is _____ _____. It is a lot of _____ to read _____ novels and try to _____ who the criminal is. It is _____ to read *Robinson Crusoe* or *The Adventures of Tom Sawyer* and _____ as if you were a _____ in the _____ as you _____ the pages. It is also a _____ to read inspirational essays. Especially, essays _____ by writers who know _____ _____ about foreign countries can _____ you _____ as _____ you _____ _____ in those places.

The _____ type is reading _____ _____. Reading newspapers and magazines _____ _____ the most _____ way to get _____. _____ a lot of books _____ the Japanese economy, the American presidential system, or the _____ of infectious _____ is a way to _____ knowledge and information. This type _____ _____ _____ not be _____, but it is _____ for writing _____ and giving a presentation at a _____. _____, it is a _____ type of reading for _____ highly _____. Therefore, _____ people go to libraries and bookstores to _____ _____ _____ with various information and _____, and try to _____ a lot _____ reading them.

Finally, the _____ type is reading _____ _____ your ability to _____ youreself and _____ the size of your vocabulary. _____ you come across an expression you've _____ read _____, you can _____ a note of it, _____ it, and use it to _____ your writing _____ the next time you _____ _____. This type of reading _____ _____ _____ what the author means in a _____ way and _____ you the _____ to summarize your own _____ on it. This type of reading is _____ _____ to higher _____ in Japanese tests. _____, if you _____ _____ on the first and second types of reading, your test scores _____ _____ be as _____ as you _____ them to be.

リーディングの勉強法や
モチベーションの上げ方を
知りたい人はこちら▶ ▶ ▶
https://tb.sanseido-publ.co.jp/gakusan/mainichi-r/

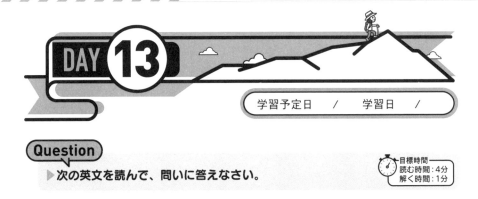

学習予定日　／　　学習日　／

Question

▶次の英文を読んで、問いに答えなさい。

目標時間
読む時間：4分
解く時間：1分

The Martian Way and Other Stories is a novel written by Isaac Asimov in 1952 about a plan to migrate to Mars, and Elon R. Musk, the founder of the space company SpaceX, said during an international space conference in Mexico in September 2016 "I want moving to Mars to be a feasible goal," announcing that he was extremely serious about his plans to move to Mars. In addition to him, there have been many scientists who have proposed a move to Mars, and the term "terraforming" was used as a term to describe artificially modifying the environment of Mars to a level close to that of the Earth and making it habitable for humans and other organisms.

Why do we need to migrate? For one thing, the Earth is experiencing a population explosion, which will cause a food crisis in the future. There is also the undeniable possibility that air and water pollution will make the Earth uninhabitable for humans. Therefore, it is necessary to create an environment where humans can live on other planets.

The rotation period of Mars is almost 24 hours, just like the Earth, and the axial tilt angle is about 25 degrees, similar to our planet, which means there are four seasons. For these reasons, the plan to move to Mars has been conceived. However, the temperature on Mars is much lower than on the Earth, at about minus 40 degrees Celsius, and the surface is covered with hard ice. There is no water or oxygen, so it is necessary to create them artificially. Astronomer Carl Sagan suggested in 1971 that carbon dioxide gas could be generated by melting the ice near the poles of Mars, and in 1991, scientist Chris McKay stated in a paper published in the journal *Nature* that a suitable atmosphere could be created if Mars had carbon dioxide and nitrogen.

However, unfortunately, a paper by an American research team published in 2018 concluded that existing science and technology makes it almost impossible to make Mars a habitable environment for humans. Elon R. Musk himself said at a virtual summit in August 2020, "There is no doubt that the first settlers will die on Mars." But when a private Dutch organization established with the goal of creating the first human extraterrestrial colony on Mars began accepting applications for prospective settlers in 2013, a flood of applicants applied for a one-way ticket to spend the rest of their lives on Mars. Would you be interested in applying for the project to move to Mars?

（注）feasible 達成可能な　　terraforming 惑星地球化

　　　axial tilt angle 地軸傾斜角　　extraterrestrial 地球外の

Q 次の①〜⑤の英文が本文の内容に一致している場合は T、一致していない場合は F を（　）内に書き入れなさい。

① Elon R. Musk is the first person to express the idea of moving to Mars.

（　　　）

② Humanity may not be able to live on the Earth due to the population explosion and pollution.

（　　　）

③ Mars is close to the Earth, and if we can raise the temperature, we can get oxygen and water.

（　　　）

④ Musk himself has stated that it would be impossible for humans to live on Mars.

（　　　）

⑤ In 2013 many people applied for a project to move to Mars even though they would never be able to return to the Earth.

（　　　）

解答・解説

Q 解答 ①F ②T ③F ④F ⑤T

....

Q 解説

① 「イーロン・R・マスクが火星移住という考えを表した最初の人物である」という意味。第1段落第1文にアイザック・アシモフの小説が取り上げられているが、それが書かれたのが1952年であり、マスクが最初の人物ではないことがわかる。

② 「人口爆発と汚染のために、人類は地球に住めなくなるかもしれない」という意味。第2段落に the Earth is experiencing a population explosion とあり、さらに air and water pollution will make the Earth uninhabitable for humans とあることから判断する。

③ 「火星は地球に近く、温度を上げることができれば酸素と水を得ることができる」という意味。本文中には地球と火星の距離についての言及はなく、また温度を上げることで酸素や水を得られる説明もないので一致しない。

④ 「マスク自身、人類が火星に住むことは不可能だろうと述べている」という意味。第4段落にマスクの言葉として There is no doubt that the first settlers will die on Mars. が紹介されているが、火星に住むことが「不可能だろう」という記述はない。

⑤ 「決して地球に戻ることはできないにもかかわらず、2013年に火星への移住計画に多くの人が申し込んだ」という意味。最終段落に2013年に開始した募集で a flood of applicants applied for a one-way ticket to spend the rest of their lives on Mars とあるので、一致している。

英文訳

　The Martian Way and Other Stories（邦題『火星人の方法』）はアイザック・アシモフが1952年に書いた火星移住計画を主題とした小説であるが、宇宙開発企業スペースXの創設者であるイーロン・R・マスクは2016年9月にメキシコで開催された国際宇宙会議のなかで、「火星への移住が実現可能な目標になってほしい」と述べ、極めて真剣に火星への移住を計画していることを発表した。彼以外にも火星に移住することを提案してきた科学者は多数いて、火星の環境を地球環境に近い水準まで人為的に改変し、人類や他の生物が居住可能にすることを表す terraforming（惑星地球化）という言葉が用いられた。

　なぜ、われわれは移住をする必要があるのだろうか。ひとつには地球が人口爆発を起こしていて、そのために将来食糧危機が生じるという問題がある。また、大気汚染や水質汚染によって、人類が地球に住めなくなる可能性も否定できない。そこで、地球以外の惑星に人類が住める環境をつくっておく必要があるということである。

　火星の自転周期は地球と同じくほぼ24時間であり、地球に似て地軸傾斜角が約25度なので、四季が存在する。これらの理由で火星に移住する計画が考え出されたのである。しかし、火星の気温は地球よりかなり低く、およそ摂氏マイナス40度であり、表面は硬い氷におおわれている。水や酸素もないので、人工的に作り出す必要がある。天文学者のカール・セーガンは1971年に、火星の両極付近の氷を溶かして炭酸ガスを発生させることができると提案した。1991年には、科学者のクリス・マッケイが専門誌『ネイチャー』に掲載された論文において、火星に二酸化炭素と窒素があれば、適した大気を創出することは可能だと述べている。

　しかし残念ながら、2018年に発表されたアメリカのある研究チームの論文によると、既存の科学技術では火星を人類が暮らせるような環境にすることはほとんど不可能であると結論づけられている。マスク自身、2020年8月に行われた仮想サミットで「最初の移住者たちが火星で亡くなることは間違いないだろう」と発言している。しかし、火星に人類初の地球外植民地をつくることを目的として設立されたオランダの民間組織が、入植希望者の募集を2013年に開始した際、火星で生涯を終えるための片道切符に応募者が殺到した。あなたは火星への移住プロジェクトに応募したいと思うだろうか。

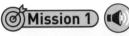

Mission 1 🔊

▶ Question の英文を見ながら、音読トレーニングをしよう。

音読トレーニング ▶ ☐ ☐ ☐ ☐ ☐ ☐ ☐ ☐ ☐ ☐

Mission 2

▶ 前ページの英文訳を見ながら、バックトランスレーションをして、内容を
しっかりマスターできたか確認しよう。

The Martian Way and Other Stories is a ＿＿＿ ＿＿＿ by Isaac
Asimov ＿＿＿ 1952 ＿＿＿ a plan to ＿＿＿ to Mars, and Elon R. Musk,
the ＿＿＿ of the ＿＿＿ company SpaceX, said ＿＿＿ an international
＿＿＿ ＿＿＿ in Mexico in September 2016 "I want ＿＿＿ to ＿＿＿ to be
a feasible goal," announcing that he was ＿＿＿ ＿＿＿ about his
＿＿＿ to ＿＿＿ to Mars. ＿＿＿ ＿＿＿ to him, there have been many
scientists who ＿＿＿ ＿＿＿ a ＿＿＿ to Mars, and the ＿＿＿ "terraforming"
was ＿＿＿ as a ＿＿＿ to ＿＿＿ artificially modifying the environmnet
of ＿＿＿ to a ＿＿＿ ＿＿＿ to that of the Earth and ＿＿＿ it habitable
＿＿＿ ＿＿＿ and other ＿＿＿.

＿＿＿ do we ＿＿＿ to migrate? For ＿＿＿ ＿＿＿, the Earth is
experiencing a ＿＿＿ ＿＿＿, which will ＿＿＿ a food ＿＿＿ in the ＿＿＿.
There is ＿＿＿ the undeniable ＿＿＿ that ＿＿＿ and water ＿＿＿ will
＿＿＿ the Earth uninhabitable for ＿＿＿. ＿＿＿, it is necessary to
＿＿＿ an environment ＿＿＿ humans ＿＿＿ ＿＿＿ on other planets.

The rotation ＿＿＿ of Mars is ＿＿＿ 24 ＿＿＿, just like the ＿＿＿,

and the axial tilt ____ is about 25 ____, similar to our ____, which ____ there are four ____. For these ____, the ____ to ____ to Mars has been conceived. However, the ____ on Mars is ____ ____ than on the Earth, at about ____ 40 degrees Celsius, and the ____ is ____ with hard ____. There is ____ ____ or oxygen, so it is necessary to ____ them artificially. Astronomer Carl Sagan ____ in 1971 that ____ dioxide gas ____ be generated ____ ____ the ice near the ____ of Mars, and in 1991, ____ Chris McKay stated in a paper ____ in the journal *Nature* that a ____ atmosphere could be ____ if Mars had carbon dioxide and nitrogen.

However, ____, a paper by an American ____ ____ published in 2018 ____ that existing science and technology makes it almost ____ to ____ Mars a ____ environment for ____. Elon R. Musk himself ____ at a virtual ____ in August 2020, "There is ____ ____ that the ____ settlers will ____ on Mars." But when a private Dutch organization ____ with the ____ of creating the ____ human extraterrestrial colony ____ Mars ____ accepting applications ____ prospective ____ in 2013, a ____ of applicants ____ for a one-way ____ to ____ the ____ of their ____ on Mars. Would you ____ ____ in applying for the ____ to ____ to Mars?

リーディングの勉強法や
モチベーションの上げ方を
知りたい人はこちら▶▶▶
https://tb.sanseido-publ.co.jp/gakusan/mainichi-r/

Question

▶次の英文を読んで、問いに答えなさい。

目標時間
読む時間：4分
解く時間：1分

A Japanese musician wrote in his essay that there are indeed things more important than money, but you need money to get those important things. To be sure, in order to get those things, you need some, if not a lot of, money. In this respect, the musician has a point.

Many people may hope to earn a lot of money, but they do not know what to do to realize their goal. Schools may teach English and mathematics, but not how to make money. Universities teach economics, but not how to become rich. Therefore, ordinary people tend to think all they have to do is work hard. But is it possible to become rich if you work from morning till night? The answer is no. How can you make money in order to get something more important than money?

First, you have to study. Whether it's English, math, baseball, music, whatever, you need to raise your level and create something that other people can't beat. Would you pay money for a boring movie? People are willing to pay for something of a high level. If you create something that is second to none, people won't hesitate to spend money on you. The only way to raise your level is to study. Don't forget studying is an economic activity to make money.

The second is to be original. Successful people start by imitating, but they think for themselves, create their own style, and produce something that can't be made anywhere else. If Steve Jobs had created the iPhone or Macintosh computer by copying another company's product, he would not have been so successful. Look at other people who have succeeded in life and think about what you can do and what you can create.

The third thing, and maybe the most important thing, is to contribute to other people and society. Great novelists or filmmakers contribute to society by creating inspiring works. Top athletes and musicians contribute to society by inspiring people with their great performances. IT company executives contribute to society by delivering great products that make society more convenient. Even if you have graduated from a top university, if you cannot contribute to other people, who will give you any money?

If you remember these three points, you can make money. Don't try to make money. Raise your level, be creative, and contribute to society, and money will naturally come to you. Money is a result, not a goal.

Q 次の①～⑤の英文が本文の内容に一致している場合は T、一致していない場合は F を（　）内に書き入れなさい。

① A Japanese musician says there is nothing more important than money, which is right.

（　　　）

② High schools and universities don't teach students how to make money, but that is a wrong approach to education.

（　　　）

③ If you don't study hard and improve yourself, you will not be able to make money.

（　　　）

④ Originality is not something you learn from others, so it is important to imitate others.

（　　　）

⑤ Even highly capable people cannot make money if they do not contribute to society.

（　　　）

解答・解説

Q 解答 ①F ②F ③T ④F ⑤T

··

Q 解説

① 「日本のミュージシャンがお金ほど大切なものはないと言っているが、それは正しい」という意味。第1段落で音楽家の発言として書かれているのは there are indeed things more important than money, but you need money to get those important things ということであるので、一致していない。

② 「高校と大学では生徒にお金の稼ぎ方を教えないが、それは間違った教育方法である」という意味。第2段落に学校と大学でお金の稼ぎ方や金持ちになる方法を教えないという記述はあるが、「間違った教育方法」という記述はない。

③ 「一生懸命勉強せず、自分を高めなければ、お金を稼ぐことなどできないだろう」という意味。第3段落で First, you have to study. とあり、続いて you need to raise your level とあることから判断すれば、内容に一致している。

④ 「独創性は他人から教わるものではないので、他人を真似ることが大切である」という意味。第4段落で Successful people start by imitating, but they think for themselves とはあるが、他人から教わるものではないとも、真似ることが大切だとも書かれていない。

⑤ 「能力の高い人でさえも、社会に貢献しないのであれば、お金を稼ぐことはできない」という意味。第5段落で Even if you have graduated from a top university, if you cannot contribute to other people, who will give you any money? とあり、一致している。

英文訳

　ある日本のミュージシャンが、確かにお金より大切なものはあるが、その大切なものを手に入れるためにはお金が要ると、自分のエッセイに書いていた。確かに、それらを手に入れるためには、大金ではないにしてもいくらかのお金は必要であり、その点でそのミュージシャンの考え方には一理ある。

　多額のお金を稼ぎたいと思っている人は多いかもしれないが、彼らは自らの目標をかなえるために何をすればよいのかを知らない。学校では英語や数学を教えるかもしれないが、お金の稼ぎ方は教えない。大学は経済学を教えているが、お金持ちになるための方法は教えていない。したがって、ふつうの人は、一生懸命に働きさえすればよいと考えがちである。しかし朝から晩まで働けば、お金持ちになれるのであろうか。答えはノーである。お金より大切な何かを手に入れるために、どうすればお金を稼ぐことができるのであろうか。

　まずは、勉強することである。英語でも数学でも野球でも音楽でも何でもよいので、自分のレベルを上げ、他の人には負けない何かをつくることである。あなたはつまらない映画に対してお金を払おうとするだろうか。人はレベルの高いものに対して、お金を払いたいのである。誰にも負けない何かをつくれば、人々はあなたにお金を使うことをためらわない。自分自身のレベルを上げるためには勉強をするしかない。勉強はお金を稼ぐための経済活動であることを忘れてはならない。

　次に、独創的であるということである。成功している人たちは、模倣をすることから始めるが、自分で考え、自分のスタイルをつくり、他のどこにもないものを創造する。もし、スティーブ・ジョブズが他社製品を真似て iPhone やマッキントッシュコンピュータを創っていたら、こんなにも成功しなかっただろう。人生で成功している他の人たちを見て、自分には何ができるのか、何を創り出せるのかを考えることである。

　三番目は、そしておそらく一番大切なことは、他の人々や社会に貢献するということである。偉大な小説家や映画監督は、感動的な作品を創造することで社会に貢献する。一流のアスリートや音楽家は、素晴らしいパフォーマンスで人々を感動させることで社会に貢献する。IT 企業の経営者たちは、より便利な社会をつくる素晴らしい製品を送り出すことで社会に貢献する。あなたが一流大学を出ていたとしても、他者に貢献できなければ、誰があなたにお金を払うだろうか。

　これら3つの点を忘れなければ、お金を稼ぐことができる。お金を儲けようとしてはならない。自分のレベルを上げ、独創的であり、社会に貢献すれば、自然とお金がやってくるのである。お金は結果であり、目的ではない。

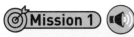Mission 1 🔊

▶ **Question の英文を見ながら、音読トレーニングをしよう。**

音読トレーニング ➤ □ □ □ □ □ □ □ □ □ □

Mission 2

▶前ページの英文訳を見ながら、バックトランスレーションをして、内容を
しっかりマスターできたか確認しよう。

A Japanese _____ wrote in his _____ that there are _____ things more _____ than _____, but you need _____ to get those _____ things. _____ _____ _____, in order to _____ those things, you _____ some, if _____ a lot of, money. In this _____, the musician has a _____.

Many people _____ _____ to _____ a lot of money, but _____ do not _____ _____ to do to _____ their goal. Schools may _____ English and mathematics, _____ not _____ _____ make money. Universities _____ economics, but not _____ _____ become _____. Therefore, ordinary people _____ _____ think all they have to _____ is _____ _____. But is it _____ to become _____ if you _____ from morning _____ night? The _____ is _____. How can you _____ _____ in order to get something more _____ than _____?

_____, you have to study. _____ it's English, math, _____, music, _____, you need to _____ your _____ and _____ something that _____ people can't _____. Would you _____ money for a _____ _____? People are _____ _____ pay for something of a _____ level. If you _____

90

something that is ____ to ____, people won't ____ to spend ____ on you. The ____ ____ to ____ your level is to ____. Don't ____ studying is an ____ activity to make money.

The ____ is to ____ ____. ____ people start by ____, but they ____ for themselves, create their own ____, and ____ something that can't be ____ anywhere else. ____ Steve Jobs had ____ the iPhone or Macintosh computer by ____ another company's product, he ____ not have been so ____. Look at other people who have succeeded ____ ____ and think about ____ ____ ____ do and ____ you can ____.

The ____ thing, and ____ the ____ important thing, is to ____ to other people and ____. Great novelists or filmmakers contribute to ____ by creating ____ ____. Top athletes and musicians ____ to society by ____ people with their ____ ____. IT company executives contribute to society by ____ great ____ that make society more ____. Even if you ____ ____ from a top university, if you ____ ____ to other people, who will ____ you any ____?

If you ____ these ____ points, you can ____ money. Don't try to make money. ____ your level, ____ ____, and contribute to ____, and money will ____ come to you. Money is a ____, not a ____.

リーディングの勉強法や
モチベーションの上げ方を
知りたい人はこちら▶▶▶
https://tb.sanseido-publ.co.jp/gakusan/mainichi-r/

Review 2   DAY 8〜14で学習した単語や表現を復習しよう。

☐	atmosphere	名	（天体を取り巻く）大気	▶ DAY 13
☐	gain	動	手に入れる、獲得する	▶ DAY 12
☐	contribute	動	貢献する	▶ DAY 14
☐	disease	名	病気、疾患	▶ DAY 9
☐	artificially	副	人為的に	▶ DAY 13
☐	perspective	名	観点、視点	▶ DAY 10
☐	generally	副	概して、一般的に	▶ DAY 8
☐	modify	動	変更する、修正する	▶ DAY 13
☐	curiously	副	興味ありげに、物珍しそうに	▶ DAY 11
☐	strengthen	動	強める、強化する	▶ DAY 10
☐	incorrect	形	間違った、不正確な	▶ DAY 11
☐	feature	名	特徴、特色	▶ DAY 8
☐	be willing to 〜		〜する意志がある	▶ DAY 14
☐	prohibit	動	禁止する	▶ DAY 9
☐	conceive	動	考えつく	▶ DAY 13
☐	properly	副	適切に、きちんと	▶ DAY 11
☐	improve	動	改善する、上達させる	▶ DAY 12
☐	purpose	名	目的、意図	▶ DAY 9
☐	creature	名	生き物、生物	▶ DAY 10
☐	migrate	動	移住する、移動する	▶ DAY 13
☐	emphasize	動	強調する	▶ DAY 8
☐	educated	形	教養のある	▶ DAY 12
☐	excessive	形	過度の、極端な	▶ DAY 9
☐	to be sure		確かに	▶ DAY 14
☐	treat	動	扱う、待遇する	▶ DAY 11

コラム 2 ～筆者の主張を正確につかむことが最終目標！～

　浪人して予備校に通っていたころ、構造分析をしながら読むという武器を
手に入れました。主語はこれ、動詞はこれといった具合に読んでいくこと
で、英文を丸裸にできます。修飾関係を見抜いたときには、まるで難解なパ
ズルを解読したかのような気持ちになり、構造分析こそが英語を読む醍醐味
だと信じこんでいた時期があります。

　灘校の同僚たちと金沢に旅行したことがあります。電車の中で物理の先生
が洋書を取り出し、読み始めました。ビールをおいしそうに飲みながら、
けっこうな速度で読み進めておられます。「洋書がお好きなんですか」と尋
ねますと「この推理小説、面白いよ」とのこと。「文構造とか単語とか難し
い箇所はありますか」と問いますと「文構造なんか意識していると読めない
じゃないか」というお返事でした。その先生は金沢までの2時間で、その小
説のほとんどを読んでしまわれました。

　この「文構造なんか意識していると読めない」ということに気づくと速く
読めるようになります。確かに初期段階では構造を意識することは大切で
す。しかし、いつまでも構造ばかりを追いかけていると、文章の内容が頭に
入ってこないはずです。信じられないという人は、日本語の本でやってみて
ください。すべての単語にSだのVだのを記入しながら読んでみてくださ
い。読み終わる頃には、中身がほとんどまったく理解できていないことがわ
かるはずです。

　構造分析をしながら読むのは、初期段階では大切です。でも、高校2年生
や3年生になって、いよいよ大学入試に向かおうとするときに、構造ばかり
を追いかけていると、速く読むことも、筆者の言いたいことを理解すること
もかなり難しくなります。下線部だけは構造を意識して、しっかりと解答す
るにしても、それ以外の部分については読み飛ばしていくという、いわば強
弱をつけた読み方ができるようになれば、皆さんの英語の成績は驚くほど伸
びるはずです。習慣がそれを可能にしますので、毎日続けてくださいね。

●著者紹介

木村達哉

1964年1月29日生まれ。奈良県出身。関西学院大学文学部英文学科卒業。西大和学園教諭として10年間教鞭をとったあと、灘中学校・高等学校に赴任。教員以外にも、執筆業やチームキムタツを運営するなど多方面で活躍。趣味は料理とダイエット。また、野球が好きで、灘校に赴任して以来、野球部の顧問を務めている。主な著書は『キムタツ・シバハラの 英作文、対談ならわかりやすいかなと思いまして。』(三省堂)、『ユメタン』シリーズ（アルク）など多数。

デ ザ イ ン	米倉八潮 (Vsigns Graphic 合同会社)
イ ラ ス ト	オオノマサフミ
撮　　　影	株式会社メディアパートメント (杉野正和)
録　　　音	株式会社巧芸創作
英 文 校 閲	Freya Martin
編 集 協 力	福本健太郎・久松紀子
D　T　P	亜細亜印刷株式会社
協　　　力	チームキムタツ

毎日続ける！　英語リーディング2　速読編

2021年3月31日　第1刷発行

著　者　　　木村達哉

発行者　　　株式会社三省堂
　　　　　　代表者 瀧本多加志

印刷者　　三省堂印刷株式会社

発行所　　　株式会社三省堂

〒101-8371 東京都千代田区神田三崎町二丁目22番14号
電話 編集 (03) 3230-9411
営業 (03) 3230-9412
https://www.sanseido.co.jp/